Potato City

Potato City

Nature, History,
and Community
in the Age of Sprawl

SUE LEAF

Borealis Books is an imprint of the
Minnesota Historical Society Press.

www.borealisbooks.org

The Minnesota Historical Society Press
is a member of the Association of
American University Presses.

Manufactured in the United States of America

10 9 8 7 6 5 4 3 2 1

∞ The paper used in this publication meets the
minimum requirements of the American National Standard for Information Sciences—Per-
manence for Printed Library Materials, ANSI
Z39.48-1984.

International Standard Book Number
0-87351-507-2 (cloth)

Library of Congress
Cataloging-in-Publication Data

Leaf, Sue, 1953–
    Potato City : nature, history, and community
in the Age of Sprawl / Sue Leaf.
        p.   cm.
    ISBN 0-87351-507-2 (cloth : alk. paper)
    1.   North Branch (Minn.)—History.
    2.   North Branch (Minn.)—
         Social conditions.
    3.   Community life—Minnesota—
         North Branch.
    4.   Potato growers—Minnesota—
         North Branch—History.
    5.   North Branch (Minn.)—Environmental
         conditions.
    6.   Natural history—Minnesota—
         North Branch.
    7.   Nature—Effect of human beings on—
         Minnesota—North Branch.
    8.   Human ecology—Minnesota—
         North Branch.
    9.   Cities and towns—Minnesota—
         Growth—Case studies.
    10. Suburbs—Environmental aspects—
         Minnesota—Case studies.
    I.   Title.
    F614.N58L43 2004
    977.6'61—dc22   2004006335

Poem on page 8 from
    Ride a Purple Pelican by Jack Prelutsky. Used
    by permission of HarperCollins Publishers.
Poem on page 19 appeared in the
    North Branch Review on April 6, 1894
Quotation on page 176 from
    A Sand County Almanac (Oxford:
    Oxford University Press, 1989), 148–49

Potato City

Preface

EVERY PLACE HAS A HISTORY. This is a truism so
commonplace as to be almost trite—almost, but not quite, because
so few Americans really know the history of the place where they
live. A place's history can be understood on a long scale, its geologic
past, or on a short scale, its human history. Somewhere in between,
existing concurrently with the geologic and human pasts, is a
place's natural history, an account of its nonhuman life. All of these
histories speak to the present.

When I moved to North Branch, Minnesota, and, later, when I sat
down to write this book, I was driven by simple curiosity about the
town's past. I could see relics from a former life in my walks about
town—trees I thought had not been planted, shaggy prairie grasses
poking up in "civilized" spots, aged buildings that had not been dis-
guised by aluminum siding. These intrigued me. They seemed to be
ghosts, a type of memory, mute witnesses of a past life. I desired to
know more about them and to place them in a greater context.

I soon realized that by knowing my community's past I could better interpret its present, or at least detect patterns that had existed for decades. I was most interested in the intersection of human and natural history. How had North Branch's pioneers viewed the savanna? The sand plain? How have people used its natural wealth? And how has that use changed over time?

In any Minnesota community, these questions are fairly easy to answer, at least from a Euro-American perspective. Settlement here by European immigrants is a recent phenomenon; we tend to forget how recent. In piecing together North Branch's past, I worked within a 120-year frame, two or three generations' worth of time. I sought out very old residents with good memories and found that they knew some of the town's first settlers. Several nonagenarians had clear recollections of North Branch's first physician, Dr. Zeien, who came to the area in the mid-1880s and remained in practice for fifty years. This personal connection illustrated the brevity of settlement more starkly than any timeline could.

The past creates our future. This belief drives our study of history—from the level of public school curriculum to that of academic research. Seldom, though, do we study history on the miniature scale of the local community, yet that is where history has the most direct impact on our present lives. As I pieced together the fragmented past of humble, homely North Branch, I came to believe that the natural world in every place has beauty to offer, that every community, no matter how prosaic, has stories to tell.

Potato City

One

Into the Garden

I STOOD IN THE GARDEN behind the house at 721 Oak Street in North Branch, Minnesota, and studied the remains of plants that curled, dark and dry, on the soil. It was September, and the garden had been brought up short by the first killing frost. Blackened tomato plants suffering from wilt sprawled haphazardly in one corner. Small, successive mounds of overturned earth indicated that someone had been digging new potatoes. Pale, bloated, over-ripe cucumbers clung to shriveled vines. A thin line of papery cornstalks rustled softly. As I scuffed the toe of my tennis shoe through the light, grayish soil, small puffs of dust rose and drifted away. It did not seem to hold much promise for growing vegetables, though the house's owners assured us they had worked a garden in this spot for thirty years.

I had come to the garden because we were about to buy the house at 721 Oak Street. My husband had signed a contract with the North Branch Clinic, two doors east. We would move to town in two months. While Tom and our young son checked out the wiring and other mechanics of the house, I ambled my heavily pregnant self out back to see what it would reveal. Gardens, like houses, hold clues to the future, and I wondered what this garden would tell me. Would we be happy here? Would we grow and be successful? Would we bear fruit?

The day was sunny and warm. The oaks in the yard were beginning to kindle with the reds and rusts of fall, and the neighborhood was quiet, drowsy. The only sound was the background whine of the dryers on the grain elevators at Peterson's mill, several blocks away. The corn harvest was coming in to the mill, and the grain was being stored and dried before being shipped to market via either truck or rail. The golden light of the air and the continuous, high-pitched drone of the dryers lent an odd tranquility to the scene.

Scuffing the soil again, I bent down to get a better look. It was very fine, light soil, almost sandy. Sand? I tried to recall what I knew about east-central Minnesota. A large expanse of sand, the Anoka Sand Plain, stretched over a major portion of the counties just north of the Twin Cities. The sand had been deposited there ten thousand years ago as outwash from the newly formed Mississippi River. The river had drained the receding glacier, carrying its sandy residue into what is now east-central Minnesota.

Years ago, as a young graduate student in zoology at the University of Minnesota, I had live-trapped small mammals in Anoka County, the heart of the sand plain. The soil there had been almost yellow, utterly sandy, devoid of humic content. This soil was different—finer in texture and darker in color—but still sand. Could the Anoka Sand Plain extend this far east? The prospect of living on the sand plain appealed to me. It seemed a feature that could give shape and meaning to a community, like the presence of Lake Superior, or the prairie lands to the west.

It was, indeed, the eastern edge of the Anoka Sand Plain, and in the years that followed my introduction to the garden on Oak Street I came to know a great deal about sand. When the soil was dry—nearly all the time—its fine, powdery texture clung to my skin, insinuating itself into every crease and line of my feet and hands. I learned to reserve a pair of old tennis shoes just for garden work, and the soil ground itself into the canvas until it was gray.

Although our road was paved, fine sand still found its way inside the house and, odder still, into our beds. The plastic covers over the children's mattresses were continuously coated with a thin layer of grime that I periodically sponged off. It took no imagination to see how the sand sifted into the house: every farmer doing fieldwork, whether it was disking or planting, cultivating or harvesting—but especially disking in the spring, when the soil was dry—kicked up clouds of light dust that drifted away on the wind. I did not want to contemplate housekeeping conditions in homes on the many gravel roads that crisscrossed Chisago County.

I learned from my garden that, though droughty, the soil was very fertile. If I could only keep it watered in May and June—and that meant sprinkling every day it did not rain—I would harvest firm, red tomatoes, creamy yellow squash, and potatoes—lots of potatoes.

Potatoes thrive in sandy soil. Sand drains well, so the growing tubers are not constantly surrounded by waterlogged soil that can't warm—a condition promoting slow growth and even rot. I planted whatever varieties I could get at the local mill—Red Norlands or Early Ohios, for early, red-skinned potatoes; Kennebecs, with rough, pale skins, to keep through the winter. The Kennebecs, especially, could grow to enormous size. Frequently I would dig up a potato that was as large as my two fists put together. Such a potato would feed the whole family—Tom, me, and our two small children.

I also discovered that, because it drained well, the soil warmed quickly in the spring. I could work it in March and plant lettuce, radishes, and onions two weeks before gardeners who had heavier soil. Potatoes went into the ground in early April.

Planting potatoes became a family affair. Sometimes Tom helped me, but more often I enlisted one of the kids to carry the bucket of seed potatoes. Our preschoolers enjoyed the garden work. They took seriously the job of planting, following me as I spaded each hole. While I held back the soil, they placed the cut edge of the seed potato down into the earth, so the eyes would grow straight up. We'd serenade the newly planted potatoes with a favorite nonsense poem:

> *Poor potatoes underground*
> *never get to look around,*
> *do not have a chance to see*
> *butterfly or bumblebee.*
>
> *Poor potatoes never look*
> *at the fishes in the brook,*
> *never see the sunny skies—*
> *what a waste of all those eyes!*

In the fall, the children would follow me again to the garden, this time to pick up the crop of potatoes as I forked open each hill. It was magic! From each small piece of potato they had poked into the sandy earth in the spring there had risen five or six large, full potatoes in September. It never failed to impress the three-year-olds—or me.

In the months between planting and harvest, I watered, cultivated, and fertilized the plants, mounding soil over the swelling tubers when they pushed their way to the surface, creating little hills. Some summers, potato beetles attacked the green, growing plants. Maddeningly attractive, with hard, black-and-white-striped shells, the beetles would fly into my nicely thriving patch, lay their tiny orange eggs inconspicuously on the underside of the plants' leaves, and disappear. When the eggs hatched, the orange and black larvae would begin eating potato leaves, each successive instar larger and more voracious than the last.

It took one season for me to learn that potato beetles could not be ignored. I became watchful for adult beetles as July approached. I was not alone in my vigilance. I could pick up information about the advent of beetles any time I walked up town: in the post office, in the grocery store, over coffee in the bakery. North Branch gardeners were alert for potato beetles, and it was a topic of considerable interest.

If I saw even one in my garden, I popped it into a discarded glass jar, where it would die a deserved, lingering death. Then I'd search anxiously for the hidden eggs. I'd rub out the egg masses by hand, my fingers staining yellow in the process. But I didn't care. I was ruthless. A week or two later, I would begin destroying larvae. At first I was squeamish about squishing them—they made a much bigger squish than the eggs and, besides, larvae *wiggled*—but soon I became inured to even that, a hard-nosed gardener protecting the potato crop.

Although I did not know it, I was recapitulating history in my little garden on Oak Street. North Branch had once been the hub of a thriving potato industry, around which the town and the surrounding farms revolved.

The snug downtown area showed no evidence that North Branch had once been Pot-8-O City (as early local newspapers referred to it). The potato starch factories, which had kicked out tons of product each year, had vanished without a trace. The Splittstoser Company, manufacturing farm implements and shipping them all over the Upper Midwest, had likewise disappeared. The square, brown brick building that had been Splittstoser property remained on the edge of town, looking seedy and decayed and housing a small automotive shop. The train station, the scales that weighed potatoes, the "pit" in which prices were established and deals struck, the warehouses that stored millions of bushels of spuds—everything connected to potatoes was gone by 1984, when we moved to town.

In conversation, our new friends and neighbors, eager to acquaint us with the town, mentioned the potatoes in passing. "Potatoes were once really big around here," they'd say. "Shipped them out on the railroad." But these were people our age, raised in the latter half of the century. Potato stories had assumed in their minds the stature of myth—significant but nebulous, lacking in detail.

My first few years in North Branch were the longest stretch of time I'd spent as an adult in any one place. It was the first time I'd ever had enough experience with a home to wonder how it had changed over time. How had it gotten from wild oak savanna to its tame cultivated state? How did people think about the natural world in which they had settled? And where did the potatoes fit in?

I devoured the brief accounts of North Branch's history that were compiled in church anniversary booklets and family collections, but these were patchy, serving only to tantalize me. Nothing of broad scope had been written about the small, modest community of North Branch. So, inspired by friends who had perused the microfilm copies of old newspapers to research their family's history, one day I sat down at the microfilm reader in our local library to recover North Branch's past.

Potato City

THE BLACK-AND-WHITE PHOTO I hold in my hand
enchants me. It depicts the construction of a railway across the oak
savanna of the Anoka Sand Plain. The photographer centered his
focus on the massive draft horses that carved out the roadbed, but
I am captivated by what appears in the background: an open, airy
landscape of tall, scraggly prairie grass dotted by wispy, evenly
spaced oak trees. It looks inviting, like an untamed park. I imagine
running unencumbered through the oaks, barefoot, hair flying,
feeling both the freedom and expanse of a prairie and the cool
shade of trees. I can't take my eyes off the photo.

This appealing landscape was what early settlers saw when
they arrived at North Branch Station in the 1870s. The community
had sprung up at the point where the newly constructed Lake Superior and Mississippi Railroad crossed the north branch of the
Sunrise River. Named after the pretty little river that gurgled and
sparkled over a sandy bed through the parklike savanna, the town

was platted in 1870, attracting settlers from nearby communities who originally had come to Minnesota from New England and up-state New York. Later, in the fall of 1870, the U.S. government established a post office at North Branch Station, further promoting its development as a thriving town.

The early residents must have been as entranced by the oaks as I was, because they deliberately preserved as many as they could. The effect was charming. In between the clapboard houses and false-fronted downtown businesses grew the dark, gnarled oaks, their tough, leathery leaves creating lacy patterns of shade on the ground. Visitors noted the town's "very pleasant appearance."

The savanna land was cheap—$2.50 to $4.00 per acre—and, because of the sparsely scattered oaks, more easily cleared than heavily forested areas. At least that's what an 1893 letter printed on the front page of the *North Branch Review* claimed. But wresting the sturdy bur oaks, with their deep taproots, from the soil was grueling work for men and horses. Every cleared acre transformed from natural savanna to agricultural field—"improved," they called it—was a monument to single-minded determination.

As in most other early agricultural communities in Minnesota, the first farmers planted wheat, which had been the great cash crop since the state's territorial days. Farmers could get rich on wheat, but more often than not they reaped disappointment, not wealth. Grasshoppers, drought, bad seed, and fungal disease caused wheat crops to fail, and the grain easily exhausted the sand plain's sandy soil. By the 1880s, as the rest of Minnesota grew disenchanted with wheat, North Branch farmers, too, were looking for other crops to grow on the sand plain.

It took an outsider to recognize the sand's potential for growing potatoes. In the mid-1880s, a young speculator, Reuel L. Hall, arrived in east-central Minnesota to assess the region for potato farming. Acquainted with the industry in Aroostook County, Maine, Mr. Hall had big plans for Minnesota's sand lands. In 1886 he opened a potato starch factory in Anoka, Minnesota, a burgeoning community on the western edge of the Anoka Sand Plain, and convinced farmers that potatoes would be a profitable cash crop. Three years later, he erected two starch factories on the eastern edge of the sand plain—one in North Branch and another six miles up the railroad line at Harris.

Eighteen years after the coming of the railroad, North Branch residents became accustomed to the industrial whine of the starch factory's massive graters grinding potatoes day and night. The savanna was less quiet, but the discordance was the hum of Progress. Each year, the potato crop steadily increased as farmers forsook wheat for the brown, earthy tubers. Up and down the railroad line, stations shipped more and more carloads south to consumers. In October 1887—a full two years before the starch factories opened in North Branch and Harris—the *Rush City Post* reported farmers selling seven bushels of potatoes to every one of wheat.

The light, sandy soil gave birth to a million-dollar industry by 1892. Two years later, North Branch alone shipped out over a million bushels of spuds. The sister sand plain communities of Harris, Stacy, and Wyoming exported similar quantities. Businessmen predicted yields of five million bushels in five years. Rosy piles of red-skinned potatoes heaped in the fields or spilling over farm wagons were a common sight. They promised a life of abundance for the settlers of North Branch.

The first farms producing these vast quantities of potatoes were modest. Although a few speculators hired workers to tend large operations of one hundred or more acres, the majority of potato growers worked subsistence farms. A survey of farmers taken by the editor of the *North Branch Review* in 1893 claimed, "the experiences of the farmer in the potato belt sound like fairy tales when compared to that of the wheat raiser." Most cultivated no more than twenty acres of land and many worked only ten or fewer acres. One, John Shoberg, farming three miles west of town, stated he had earned one thousand dollars on his ten acres. "Can't complain," he commented with customary Swedish reserve.

Farmers kept much of their land in original vegetation and termed it "wild land." They cut the prairie grass as hay for livestock. They grubbed out the oaks and broke the prairie sod acre by acre if potato prices for the upcoming season looked encouraging. Bit by bit, the oak savanna disappeared.

The rise of the potato industry in North Branch occurred at a time when no one kept good records of the community's activities. Trying to piece together information is akin to peering through a glass darkly. What I glean of those early years is from newspapers of neighboring Taylors Falls and Rush City. North Branch news items were mere tidbits for these older, established communities.

The first vivid vignettes of North Branch appeared in 1891 when the *North Branch Review* began rolling off the presses. The literate pen of editor John Huber detailed the blooming industry and the changes it brought to the community. Huber believed his paper to be "simply a mirror of the events that transpire in the community," but for me it became a lens that brought into focus the bustling activities of the burgeoning town.

To facilitate commerce, the city built a small weighing house with two large platform scales alongside the railroad tracks and hired weigh masters to man it. The potato season began in August with the harvest of tender, young new potatoes. These small, thin-skinned delicacies were snapped up by local merchants or shipped to nearby Twin Cities markets.

Later in the season, beginning in September, the remainder of the potato crop, now mature, was harvested. Using horse-drawn wagons, farmers hauled large, heavy tubers to be weighed and bought by wholesalers. In the 1890s, the weigh master dealt with as many as 250 to 500 wagonloads daily. On the busiest days, at the peak of harvest, long lines of potato-filled wagons snaked through town, backed up at the scales. I try to imagine the scene: the fall sky bright blue, the patient horses stomping hooves and swishing tails against persistent flies, the jingle of the harnesses and the desultory chat of farmers, some in English, some in Swedish, some in German, as they wait their turns. Lingering grains of sand cling to the rough, brown potato skins. Grimy creases mark the men's denim workclothes. The pungency of horses and the fragrance of pipe smoke scent the air.

Once their load was weighed, farmers dickered with buyers, representatives of the wholesalers, for a price for their crop. Prices fluctuated daily, like the stock market, and depended on many things, including local quantities and supplies elsewhere in the nation, particularly in potato-growing regions on the floodplain of the Mississippi River in Illinois. In the 1890s, table potatoes were destined for the large urban centers of St. Louis and Kansas City, not Minnesota. At the harvest's peak in 1892, North Branch sent twenty railroad cars south daily, each one loaded with spuds.

By 1893, fourteen out-of-state brokerage firms had buyers in town. The buyers not only handled the purchase of the crop for their companies, they also insured that the potatoes were brought safely to market. During the winter months, in the years before insulated cars, the potatoes could freeze, and it was the buyer's job to see that they didn't. Cars carrying potatoes were lined with hay. In the center of the car, a small peat fire smoldered, creating just enough warmth to ward off freezing temperatures. November through March, buyers traveled south with the spuds, tending the fire. Once or twice a season, the newspaper reported a fire getting out of hand and consuming a carload of potatoes. Usually, nothing could be saved. "The loss was total," the newspaper accounts concluded.

The buyers were mostly footloose young men, free of the responsibility of wife or family, men who could afford to be out of town for days at a time. The *North Branch Review* kept townsfolk informed of their comings and goings: "Frank Colwell made his family a short call last week," the *Review* reported in January 1883. "[He] returned to Harris, ready to make his seventh trip to St. Louis with potatoes."

When in town, the buyers frequently took rooms at the local hotels. North Branch had several. James Locke ran the North Branch Hotel, conveniently connected to a livery that offered "the finest rigs in the city." Lem Quillin, a creative businessman with a colorful past as a circus clown, let out rooms at the Arlington for two dollars a day, "strictly for traveling men." Frank Olson owned the Merchant Hotel, "a first-class house in every respect." He, too, ran a livery. Association with a livery was vital for frontier hotels for the same reason that their modern counterparts often house car rental agencies.

The traveling buyers who were out and about in the great cities of the Midwest, as well as the traveling salesmen who came into town on the train, kept North Branch from becoming insular. Pop culture and fashion fads washed through the town—bicycles and bloomers one year, Victrolas the next. It was not a backwater community.

Along the town's railroad tracks, firms constructed warehouses in which the potato harvest could be kept. Frequently, the glut of harvest was so great that boxcars for shipping were simply unavailable and the potatoes had to be stored. Potatoes were also held in reserve until consumer demand farther south increased prices. The warehouses were huge, with a capacity of 25,000 bushels each, insulated with hay and heated, like the boxcars, with a small central fire. An 1894 map shows seven warehouses clustered around the tracks on the western edge of town. By 1910, there were fourteen—twelve for potato storage, one for potato starch, and one for farm implements manufactured locally. North Branch was the busiest station on the railroad line.

Not all potatoes of the sand plain were grown for the dinner table. The immense harvests produced a large number of small potatoes, or culls, that were funneled, instead, to the starch factories in town. North Branch had two. The Hall factory, built by Reuel Hall in 1889, was so successful that a group of North Branchers organized a second factory in 1892. Nearly every businessman in town contributed to the start-up capital, Swedish immigrants and East Coast natives alike. Run as a cooperative, the Farmers' Starch Factory was an immediate success, distributing a 30 percent dividend in its first year. There were more than enough potatoes to go around. In 1892, the two starch factories together produced over a ton of potato starch, but that figure was dwarfed in the years to come. In 1909, the Farmers' Starch Factory opened for a three-week run in July, to use up potatoes that had been stored in the warehouses over the winter. The output from that run alone was a whopping eighty tons of starch.

I am amazed as I read the impossibly large numbers of bushels of potatoes produced, weighed, shipped, ground, and turned into tonnage of starch, year after year. I lose a sense of proportion, trying to grapple with numbers that large pertaining to a town that small, for the population of North Branch, by the time the boom was in full flower at the turn of the twentieth century, was never more than eight hundred people.

In our age of Perma Press and wrinkle-free cotton, it is hard to appreciate the economic importance of starch before World War II. A newspaper article from 1892 estimated the *daily* consumption of starch in the United States at thousands of *tons*. Starch was used to stiffen cotton and linen and paper. North Branch's potato starch was shipped to eastern mills and printing businesses. Although starch can be produced from a wide variety of cultivated plants, potatoes were most cost effective, and potato starch factories sprang up in New England as the Industrial Age blossomed and large textile mills turned out vast quantities of fabric. The industry was confined to the northeastern states, however, until Hall started his starch factories on Minnesota's sand plain. This entrepreneurial venture paid off for him: a mere seven years after his first factory opened, his concerns were putting out three thousand tons of starch per year.

Table potatoes and potato starch were not the only direct products of the Anoka Sand Plain's potato industry. The area also became nationally known for its production of seed potatoes—the tubers that are planted to produce next year's crop. This was especially true in the southern United States, because the warm winters there made it impossible to store seed potatoes from a previous season's harvest. Seed potatoes from the sand lands were favored because they were of "straight stock," producing reliably uniform tubers. Triumphs, the variety of potato used as seed stock in the South, brought the highest price on the North Branch market.

Sand warms up quickly in the spring; water, which would keep the soil cool, doesn't adhere to the sand grains. Consequently, the sand plain also excelled in early varieties of table potatoes, those bearing earthy, evocative names: Early Ohios, Early Roses, Early Hebrons, and Rural New Yorkers. Burbank Russets, a late potato, also grew well.

It must have been supremely satisfying to raise potatoes on the sand plain in those early years. Although the area's first farmers had hailed from the East Coast, by the 1880s a wave of immigration brought large numbers of Swedes into North Branch. In their homeland, the Swedes had struggled to eke out a meager existence on poor, rocky soil. In the vast garden of the New World's Anoka Sand Plain, they were surrounded by miles and miles of light, rock-free soil. This soil, so unlike that of southern Sweden, produced an abundance of one crop—potatoes—which was nourishing, pleasing, and amenable to myriad culinary forms. After generations of hunger and want, the Swedish immigrants, working their own land, produced seemingly limitless food. No wonder the *North Branch Review* painted a rosy picture of Potato City in expectant, upbeat phrases.

By the mid-1890s, the North Branch station was the most active on the rail line. New buildings sprang up to fill in the downtown area. Stores did brisk trade. The Swedish Lutherans erected a stunning church with a steeple that soared over the town, then bought a bell worth two thousand dollars. New sidewalks made their way to every corner of the village. Townspeople could afford vacations to the Columbian Exhibition in Chicago, and some merchants even took winter breaks at the spas in West Baden, Indiana. When a fire destroyed several significant stores downtown, the city fathers immediately inquired into and purchased a state-of-the-art fire engine. The flowering of wealth inspired bad poetry, submitted to the *Review* by an exuberant farmer:

The kicker may kick with all his might
And the croaker may croak or sing,
But the Minnesota potato crop takes the cake
For potatoes here are king;
The woodsmen may work and the loafers loaf,
But the farmer sings a delightful strain,
For Minnesota potatoes are always on top,
Which means his financial gain.
Rainy Lake may boom and disappointed people roam
Until they're forced to stop
But North Branch is the place to get a good home
And raise a paying crop!

One hundred years later, I walk out to the western end of Oak Street, gaze north toward the main intersection two blocks away, and try to imagine the town at the turn of the twentieth century. In my mind's eye I see the railroad depot on the northwest corner, two general stores holding down the southern corners, and twelve warehouses filled with millions of potatoes flanking the railroad tracks. Due west are the two lumberyards. The Swedish Lutheran church steeple rises off to the northeast, and the oak trees in my yard are, at that time, perhaps as tall as I am. I try to image the background whir of the factories' graters, the whinny of horses harnessed to wagons brimming with potatoes, the calls of the buyers, the farmers, the merchants, the roar of the steam engines easing into the station. What immense good fortune—the American Dream, built on sand.

Reconstructing the Past

I EASE MY LITTLE NOVA down North Branch's Main Street on a snowy Wednesday morning. My destination is the North Branch Public Library, a small retail space nestled between Jimmy's Pizza and the Brick Inn, in what was once the only grocery store in town. The snow began over an hour ago and is falling heavily now, clogging the street and veiling anything more than a block away. On such a day, it is easy to conjure up shades from the past, and that is my pursuit this morning.

North Branch's quest for a vibrant, useful library has not always gone smoothly. Ninety years ago, a handful of citizens, spurred on by, I suspect, a newly arrived and energetic superintendent of schools, held fundraisers and gathered a small collection of donated books, including some from the State Library Commission, which constituted the town's first library. Within two months of opening, the collection's holdings had doubled. But the fledgling library had to move several times in short order and then was lost in a catastrophic fire in 1914. The only volumes saved were those on loan to readers.

Despite being uninsured, the nascent library recovered from the fire and appeared to prosper. In the 1920s, however, it foundered again, and for thirty years North Branch had only a casual lending system that eventually faded away. In 1970, Chisago County joined the East Central Regional Library System and North Branch became a bookmobile stop. In 1982, just before we moved to town, a branch library, albeit a small one, was established in a corner of the town's senior center. The present library, located in the former grocery store, is palatial in comparison. Finally, the effort to establish a substantial library, begun so long ago, seems to be coming to fruition.

I draw the Nova into my usual parking spot and slog through the swirling snow to the library's main door. For months I have been laboriously making my way through the microfilm copies of the weekly *North Branch Review*. The library has back copies of the paper's earliest editions, beginning in September 1891. In reconstructing the town's past, I have found the newspapers to be my best source. Very little has been written about North Branch's history. Because of the predominance of potato farming around the turn of the last century, I had hoped to a find a PH.D. thesis entitled something like "The Potato Industry of the Anoka Sand Plain" tucked away on a dusty shelf of a little-visited stack in one of the University of Minnesota libraries, but I have come away empty-handed.

A former superintendent of schools, G. W. Orwoll, wrote a comprehensive but abbreviated account for the 1976 U.S. bicentennial. Orwoll's history serves as an outline that I flesh out with details gleaned from the newspapers. If, as they say, God is in the details, then I have found life to be in the details, too. It matters, at least to me, exactly how the runaway horse accident took place, in what manner North Branch celebrated the Fourth of July, and whether or not there was snow for Christmas. Human life rejoices or suffers on small matters such as these.

So the *Reviews* await me. It takes as many as eight hours to read through one year's worth of newspapers on the library's dilapidated microfilm reader. North Branch inherited this wheezy machine with the cracked screen from the big Cambridge library, which had discarded it for a newer model. The screen isn't large enough to accommodate an entire page of the *Review*, so I scroll up and down, back and forth, peering beyond the crack in the screen, trying to take in the full picture.

The *Reviews* of the 1890s keep the same format, year after year. The front page has, in the left-hand column, a church, lodge, and professional directory (three churches, all Protestant; three lodges; assorted doctors and lawyers, no dentists), then, moving toward the center, some small ads for local businesses. The right-hand columns usually contain news from the individual communities the paper serves: "Harris Hustlings," "Wyoming Waifs," "Sunrise Silhouettes." North Branch City Council and Chisago County Board news is also printed on the front page, as are accounts of anything exciting that happened locally in the past week. Runaway horses feature prominently, the animals sometimes referred to as "roadsters."

On the *Review's* inner pages are sections devoted to international and national news. These usually amount to brief paragraphs, no doubt taken from items coming in over the telegraph wires. North Branchers—at least those living in town—needn't rely on the *Review* for state and national news: hot-off-the-press copies of the *St. Paul Pioneer* arrive by train each day.

One page is reserved for news items from around Minnesota— legislative business at the capitol in St. Paul, milling and shipping news from Minneapolis, tidbits from all over: Hastings's struggle to wrest the state hospital site from Anoka, the sale of pine stands on the Red Lake Indian Reservation, an outbreak of typhoid fever in Duluth. What interests me about this section is that the heartbeat of Minnesota life is already in place by the 1890s, more than a hundred years ago. The state is only thirty-some years old and already the mentally ill are sent to state hospitals in St. Peter and Fergus Falls, the state fair is held adjacent to the agricultural campus, and Hamline, Carleton, St. Olaf, and Gustavus Adolphus colleges are turning out graduates, both men and women.

Under a masthead on page five, the editor reserves several columns for editorial comments. In the 1890s, the editor is John H. Huber. Mr. Huber, who is also the *Review's* owner, is in his late thirties and evidently an enthusiastic Republican, since his newspaper exuberantly reports insider Republican gossip at the county level. He is not a native Minnesotan. Although I have yet to unearth a photograph of him, I have learned from the pages of the *Review* that he is of Irish/German descent. His father is a professor of languages at MacPherson College in Kansas, and he is close friends (I surmise) with the town's family physician, Dr. Zeien, reporting on the good doctor's personal life and poking gentle fun at his foibles. "Doc has donned his former good-natured look," he notes in one July issue, as Mrs. Zeien returned home after a week away.

Huber's newspaper reflects his educated background: his articles are factual, documented, and mostly devoid of the excessive, flowery language that marks so much of nineteenth-century journalism. In his editorials, he expresses outrage at the existence of capital punishment in Minnesota, dismay at the squandering of our native forests, and frequent skepticism over the worthiness of legislative doings in St. Paul. He is an enthusiastic booster of North Branch's burgeoning potato industry, but he urges that farmers diversify to protect themselves from the whims of a volatile market.

Perhaps the most interesting section of the *Review* is titled "North Branch News." I think of this section as containing the information I'd acquire from my neighbor as we both hang clothes out on the line each washday. It reports parties, visits, folks laid up with ailments, and weather conditions. From it I learn that North Branch people get around: professionals, like Dr. Zeien, ride the train into the Twin Cities on a regular basis, as often as once a month. Sometimes his visits are for professional purposes, but often he and his wife, Mary, hop a train to St. Paul to take in a show, like a traveling theatrical performance of *Ben-Hur*, or to Christmas shop at the big-city stores. Dentists come up from the Cities for the day to clean teeth. Fishing parties organize and take wagons and buggies out to Sunrise Lake all summer long. Axel Swenson, on his particularly fast horse, can make it to Center City, twelve miles away, in one hour.

What emerges from these pages is a sense of a tightly knit, pleasant community engaged in a common endeavor: making a life, getting ahead on the sand plain. Nearly everyone was raised elsewhere and came to town as adults. In one article, the newspaper estimates about a third of Chisago County to be Swedish immigrants. There are enough Swedish speakers, at any rate, to support a Swedish summer school held for six weeks at the Swedish Lutheran church in town. The immensely popular Lutheran pastor in the 1890s, the Reverend Eric Boman, preaches and delivers a Memorial Day speech in Swedish—but he and his wife are included in an outing to Fish Lake in "mixed" company of Yankees and Swedes, members of both groups the movers and shakers in town.

Life in North Branch in the 1890s appears fluid; no one is locked into place. For example, Lem Quillin, a former circus clown, alternately (and sometimes simultaneously) runs a hotel, owns the opera house, and operates a general merchandise store. (He is also put in charge of the "calithumpians" for the 1894 Fourth of July parade; it is unclear exactly what calithumpians are, but whether gymnastic types or horn tooters, it seems like a good role for a former clown.) The town merchants have a mix of Swedish and non-Swedish names. Many citizens are bilingual. Dr. Zeien, arriving in North Branch with the ability to speak English, German, and French, later picks up Swedish and Norwegian. If there are tensions between ethnic groups, editor Huber does not report them. (In his editorials he does lament the racial strife in the South.) One merchant, Al Bergh, owner of the Scandinavian Drugstore, specifies in a help-wanted ad that applicants must be Swedish; in a later ad, he amends that to Swedish *or* German. Perhaps this is to discourage the newly arrived Poles (Catholics!) from applying. Or maybe the patrons of his drugstore speak only Swedish and a clerk must be able to communicate with them.

In the 1890s, there are several Jewish families in town. Editor Huber notes (under North Branch News) that three men take the train to St. Paul to observe Yom Kippur. One family, the Edelsteins, is prominent and apparently well integrated into the Gentile community. The Edelsteins own a large general store, raise their children—Jacob, David, and Ruth—and eventually retire to a cottage in the Chisago Lakes area. "Jakie," a member of the first graduating class of North Branch High School, will later become an engineer, educated at MIT. Ruth will become a nationally known stage actress; in 2002 North Branch will name its high school auditorium after her.

The railroad is the lifeblood of the North Branch community. All goods are shipped in by rail: fresh apples, oranges, and bananas in winter, furniture, wagons, even draft horses. All products are shipped out by rail: potatoes, potato starch, small grains, wild hay. By train, travelers reach Duluth or the Cities in less than a day. Amazingly, on a "limited" express, which has few stops, people arrive in the Cities in about an hour—just like today's drivers.

The social scene changes with the seasons. In the fall, much of the community is preoccupied by the harvest, but traveling shows come to town and perform at Quillin's Opera House. The shows offer a wide variety of entertainment, ranging from Nashville minstrels to an evening of choral music and recitation put on by the Hamline University men's chorus. Sometimes the shows have a commercial side-interest. The arrival of a native "Indian doctor," who promises to host a show that is an "honest portrayal of Indian life, ceremonies and dances," is preceded by a week's worth of newspaper ads touting "Kickapoo Indian Medicine," guaranteed to cure a variety of ills.

A succession of dances begins in the fall. They are frequently sponsored by the town lodges, held at hotels, and include live music (of course) and often a meal. There is always a Christmas dance on the evening of December 25 and a New Year's dance. On leap year, the women organize the ball for February 29 and ask the men. In the late 1890s, a rash of more informal gatherings—"surprise parties"—overtakes the community. If the newspaper accounts can be believed, dozens of people descend on a favored individual in the early evening, commandeer the house (providing food), and host a party—sometimes on weeknights! Card games—cinch and whist—are popular at these gatherings and others.

People take the train to social events, too. When the Peninsula Hotel annex opens in Lindstrom, twenty-nine North Branchers travel south to celebrate at the ball and midnight dinner. They share the rail car with members of Palmer's military band, who perform the grand march at nine o'clock. On another occasion, members of the Knights of Pythias accept an invitation from their Pine City brethren and board the train north for an evening of socializing at the lodge on Lake Pokegama.

With the conclusion of winter and the melting of the snow, North Branchers head outside. There is a period when muddy roads confine farmers (and their potatoes) to home and towns people to the village, but it quickly passes. Sand dries out fast.

A bicycle craze hits North Branch, and the ungainly machines appear on the unpaved city streets. The fad affects men and women (presumably the younger set) alike, and women don bloomers for ease in pedaling. Editor Huber in his column expresses amusement, not scandal. I imagine him gazing out his window while at his newspaper desk, watching the energetic young maneuvering the cycles on the rutted, sandy streets, and shaking his head.

Fishing is popular, too. The most common destinations are Sunrise Lake, about nine miles south of town, and Nevers Dam, fifteen miles east, on the St. Croix River. People take horses on day trips; occasionally, couples camp out at the lake on short vacations. Huber reports the catches in the North Branch News—dozens on one occasion, one hundred bass in a single afternoon on another. And there is baseball. The North Branch Invincibles play the neighboring towns—Pine City, Harris, Sunrise, Taylors Falls. A hit-by-hit recap of the games is always printed on page one. Two popular players, Lee Quillin and pitcher Frank Isbel, will later be tapped for professional play with the Chicago White Stockings.

In August, as the first potatoes are dug and the state fair opens in St. Paul (special railroad fares for day-trippers), the summer activities wind down. The children return to school, and the starch factories, which have been dormant since the previous December, begin accepting potatoes. The sound of their immense graters can be heard all over town.

Are these the good old days? As I read through the *Reviews*, I wonder. In spring 1896, a spate of measles cases erupts in town, and the *Review* reports one baby death each week for about six weeks. The paper also informs readers of diphtheria outbreaks in Grantsburg and Princeton, typhoid fever in Duluth and Minneapolis, and an occasional cholera case. There are, of course, no antibiotics and won't be for fifty years. The doctors in town have the smallpox vaccine, the *Review* announces in 1894, which is fortunate because an epidemic is raging in Minneapolis.

In the 1890s, North Branch does not yet have environmental problems, probably because its population is still small. There is no city water or sewer, so each house has its own well and outhouse. The outhouses are inspected each spring by the health officer, Dr. Zeien. The wells are probably not deep—perhaps only five to fifteen feet, as a hand pump won't work much below that—and contamination is a risk they will face soon, since rain running through sand percolates unbelievably fast. The typhoid outbreak in Duluth is attributed to the intermingling of drinking water and sewage. Lake Superior is both the source of one and the repository of the other.

Other clues buried in the pages of the old *Reviews* reveal that the city forefathers have already set the community on the course that will produce today's dilemmas. Most of these clues are subtle, mere indications of an underlying mindset: that land is limitless, that waterways are cheap, efficient sewers, that some species ought to be eliminated, that poisons are a way to do it. They are not alone in these beliefs: they are human beings. Has any American community done differently?

Wolves are still spotted occasionally in the North Branch area in the 1890s, although it is not clear from newspaper accounts whether the animals are timber wolves or "brush wolves," a.k.a. coyotes. Editor Huber prints the rumors: a child killed by wolves north of Harris; three children attacked near Stacy; three children killed between Minneapolis and Anoka. Wolves are so numerous in 1891 that they "trot alongside farmers' wagons" and fill the night air with "long drawn-out howls and short yips." Huber advocates organizing a grand exterminating expedition, "a hunting party for howlers," to eliminate the menace. "Let's invite Twin Cities hunters," he proposes, "say, 300 men in all, to work a six to eight mile diameter circle, killing every wolf in sight." Identified as "varmints," "sheep stealers," and "mutton thieves," wolves have both state and county bounties on their hides. In 1893, Chisago County residents kill forty-four wolves and receive $415 in payments.

By the 1890s the State of Minnesota regulates fishing, but perhaps Wisconsin does not: the *Review* reports 410 trout caught on a weekend trip across the border. Game bird hunting, too, is managed with the seasons. Hunters seek prairie chickens as a favorite target, but by the nineties the birds are already scarce. Although over-hunting will contribute to the near demise of this once plentiful bird, what really exterminates the prairie chicken is the loss of its habitat: prairie land.

Wild savanna is disappearing in Chisago County in the 1890s. The wild lands are privately owned and each farmer clears his acreage as he sees fit. Often this is done several acres at a time—it is backbreaking work—as the farmer adds new potato or wheat fields to those already cleared and under cultivation. It has also been frequent practice for farmers to sell the savanna's oaks as firewood to Twin Cities markets. Who would ever think to set aside some of this land for posterity, as has already been done in Taylors Falls with the dramatic St. Croix Dalles? There seems to be no comprehensive view of the loss of this ecosystem.

Stories of spring logjams on the St. Croix tell me that Minnesotans continue to decimate the remaining northern forests, even as editor Huber reports on the closing of Mankato's sawmills because the Big Woods of southern Minnesota are gone. Farmers applying Paris green to control potato bugs each summer are adding arsenic to the underlying water table. The state legislature has already passed statutes attempting to control "noxious weeds"— European exotic species—and the starch factories are informed by the state that it is illegal to dump factory waste into the Sunrise River. Yet the town will continue depositing sewage into the river until the 1960s.

The weather reports from a century ago indicate more subtle change. Snowfalls in April and May are not uncommon. Light frosts occur in early August. Only in July can North Branch expect to be entirely frost-free. Today, an August frost would be unheard of.

I come to the end of another year on microfilm. "Merry Christmas!" the headlines on the front page read. In one paragraph, I learn that the young people of town are skating on the Sunrise, on the factory dam's flowage. I crank on the two-inch screw that serves as the handle to rewind the tape. The years fly backwards now, farther and farther into the past. I replace the cover on the machine, stand and stretch, then shrug on my jacket.

Outside the library, I blink in the bright sunlight, somehow expecting it to be dimmer. The snow has lessened, and I survey the whitened scene. There on the corner, one block away, was Dr. Zeien's office. I can almost see him in his big fur coat, medical bag in hand, striding off on a house call to tend a sick child. Across the street from where I stand was Bergh's Scandinavian Drugstore. Herreid's General Store was to my left, closer to the railroad tracks. Next door were the offices of the *Review*. John Huber, I imagine, has hung up his ink-spattered apron and left a "back in a few minutes" sign on the door. Above the downtown shops, the steeple of the old Swedish Lutheran church, now an Assembly of God congregation, rises heavenward. It all seems so real, I think to myself. The past is very present. It was not that long ago.

Pete Swanson's Potatoes

"WHEN I WAS A CHILD," my friend Doug tells me, "my father kept a small sack of Paris green high on a shelf in the corner of the shed. I remember him telling me, 'You must never, ever, touch that sack' and then he showed me what was inside—oh, the most beautiful jade color! So attractive! Years later, we took that sack and went out, way out, to the back forty, and buried it—just like that! It was arsenic, you know, and by then everyone knew that arsenic wasn't safe and you wouldn't want to put it in a *dump*—so we put it in the ground. When I think of that now ..." Doug's voice trails off and he gives a short laugh. "A while back, I heard that someone had bought that land and was eventually going to put a house on it, so I went out there and tried to find where we had buried it—but, of course, I couldn't."

The small sack of Paris green was the Swanson family's last remaining vestige of the potato era, a time when North Branch's sandy soil produced a lavish bloom of large, luscious tubers. The story of the potato era was, in the beginning, a story of poverty and deprivation in Sweden. Famine and starvation caused the Swedes to immigrate to a sparsely populated land where the soil, rich in humus and formed over thousands of years, had never been extensively cultivated by human beings.

Doug's grandfather, Pete Swanson, was typical of the Swedish immigrants that came to Chisago County. He arrived in 1880 and, like most of his countrymen also flooding the region around that time, had very little money and very few possessions. What education the immigrants could claim had been dictated by the Lutheran Church in Sweden. Most could read and write. Each immigrant family had their tale of horror. For Pete Swanson's family, life in Sweden was so meager that at times they had resorted to "bark bread"—ground tree bark mixed with rye flour—to stretch their sparse supplies. Disease, aided by malnutrition, killed five of the family's children in a fourteen-year span. Four brothers survived childhood. When the oldest one, Pete (Per), reached the age of mandatory conscription into the king's army, he decided it was time to leave.

It is a rich, wonderful irony that people accustomed to the hardship of hunger and the misery of eking out insufficient food from a stony, unyielding soil would, upon immigration, immediately be able to produce abundance from a soil utterly devoid of stones. After a short stint on a section crew for the railroad that ran through North Branch, Pete married and settled down on eighty acres south of town. Within several years, a speculator from Maine built a potato starch factory, encouraging Pete and other farmers to produce tubers on a large scale.

It is April 1911. The sky is bright blue and sunshine warms the barnyard mud that has been churned and thoroughly chewed by a winter's worth of hooves. By contrast, the interior of the barn is cool and dark as Pete Swanson fits his draft horses to the harness, readying them for the first fieldwork of spring. The horses have been brushed and curried until their dark coats gleam, a task Pete finds pleasing, as his fingers trace the smooth, silky hairs on the withers. Outside, an early meadowlark sings from the pasture behind the barn. Frantic barn swallows twitter and swoop from their nest under the eaves of the machine shed.

The horses bear personable, whimsical names—Snip and Molly—that hint at the affectionate regard in which they're held. Molly has a white blaze in the shape of a dollar sign on her forehead; Snip's forelock has been buzzed into a butch. They are stolid animals, large and broad-backed, stamping and shifting their weight as Pete moves his hands over their backs and bellies, adjusting straps, tightening cinches. This spring ritual, which Pete has performed for more than thirty years, is, this time, an act of faith more than anything else. Last year's rainfall amounted to no more than twelve inches, little more than a desert receives, and his crops had failed. It was the driest year ever recorded by white settlers, and Pete watched first his rye and oats, then the potatoes, shrivel and die in the fields.

Nineteen ten had, in fact, been a tough year all around. The drought began early in the spring, and the first hay crop failed. Time and again North Branchers were treated to the exasperating experience of seeing rain clouds form on the horizon, circle around, and pass by without releasing badly needed moisture. In the fall, fires raced through the tinder-dry marshes, destroying the wild hay that farmers had counted on to maintain their livestock through the coming winter. Without the wild hay, many farmers subsequently sold their milk cows rather than see them starve. Thus, the community's dream of establishing a dairy industry in the region had begun to fade.

The drought continued into 1911, marked by more wildfires and sandstorms. At times the spring winds whipped the light soil into the atmosphere so thoroughly that it darkened the sun. Off toward the horizon, it often appeared as if rain were imminent, when actually only soil hung in the air.

But on this April morning, as Pete leads the team into the farmyard, the day is sunny and nature smiles benignly on the farmer. The field to be readied for potatoes was turned over the previous fall. This morning, Pete will pass over the field with a harrow to break up the clods of earth that hardened under the winter's snows. Later, the team will pull a drag-tooth harrow through the soil, combing the land smooth and level. The field is small—ten acres—but the numerous repetitions across it and the slow pace of the horses give a man plenty of time to think. It is quiet, somewhat melodious work—the jingle of the harness's metal parts, the clink of the trace chains, the shush of the harrow's steel meeting sand, the spring songs of birds pursuing a directive to breed and produce young.

Once the field is carefully prepared, groomed as meticulously as one might comb through the fine, blond hair of a child, Pete will mark the field for planting. A homemade marker, heavily weighted and pulled by two horses, leaves parallel impressions on the silky, fine-particled soil. When the marker passes over the field a second time, perpendicular to the first marking, it creates a grid. Pete and his children, who will be recruited from the classroom for spring planting, will walk the grid, blue-and-white canvas sacks filled with cut seed potatoes slung over their shoulders, planting with hand-held planters. Years later, the fresh smell of newly turned earth, warming in the sun, and the dull, metallic-sounding *clunk* of the planter releasing the seed into the soil will bring back memories of April mornings spent in the field.

In late May 1911, the drought finally breaks. Enough rain falls to green the fields and replenish the marshes. A band of gypsies, traveling in colorful wagons, passes through town, telling fortunes, trading horses, and entertaining the townspeople with street antics. But out on the farm, the press of fieldwork leaves no time for gypsies. The seed has sent out shoots, and the robust dark green of young potato plants now dots the fields. Even before the festive Midsummer celebration on June 24, however, weeds threaten to usurp the farm. Now, in the heat of summer, Pete's precise planting pays off. Laid out as it is, the field can be cultivated both ways, up and down, back and forth.

Cultivation began in May when the emerging plants were two inches high, and Pete will cultivate two more times in the summer. The first round of cultivation went lengthwise down the field; the second, crosswise. On the third round, with a slightly larger implement, the potato plants will be "hilled up," that is, mounds of soil will be pushed against the plants to prevent the burgeoning tubers from breaking through and becoming green and bitter.

The weeds don't stand a chance, yet it is tedious work. In the early days of the farm, Pete walked behind a single-horse cultivator. The rounded hind end of the animal, glistening with sweat, was his chief view. These days, he views the hindquarters from the perch of a sulky cultivator pulled by a team. Riding in splendor, he keeps his boots out of the gritty soil, but a riding cultivator still weeds only one row. It saves walking, but not time. He rests the team occasionally in the shade of the lone bur oak on the edge of the field. Like seasoned athletes, the horses have had to ease into their summer work after a winter's respite from hard labor.

The potato bugs arrive on schedule during the first week of July. Checking his plants at the end of each day, Pete discovers first one, then several. As the attractive striped beetles scurry to the underside of the leaves, Pete thinks ahead to the next few days, realizing it's time for Paris green. People growing potatoes in small plots for home use might pick the destructive pests off by hand, but potato farmers have used Paris green for years, finding it extremely effective against potato bugs. An arsenic-based compound, the insecticide is a brilliant emerald hue. "Paris" refers to its use as a paint pigment, originally manufactured in France. It sounds exotic, but Paris green is commonplace. Anderson's drugstore in town carries large supplies and runs special sales in May, in preparation for the bug invasion. Pete mixes the bright green powder with water and applies it using a horse-drawn sprayer.

On the morning of the fifth of July, Pete wheels the heavy, cast-iron sprayer from behind the barn for its first run of the summer.

He had considered spraying before the family picnic the day before, a common tradition, but an overcast sky, and then rain, caused him to postpone his plans. Paris green washes off with rain; spraying would have been an exercise in futility. The kids were happy about this turn of events. Too often they had arrived late to the Fourth of July picnic, finding the feast picked over and lacking.

The sprayer is an old implement, bought in the nineties and in continuous use ever since. Sturdy and well designed, the machine was purchased from the local Splittstoser Company at a time when old man Splittstoser himself oversaw the manufacture of each one. The company has grown in the last twenty years. Sprayers are now shipped out by the carload all over the Upper Midwest, and in busy times, like the months preceding the growing season, the company employs ten or twelve men. Pete runs his hands over the lean, functional lines of the sprayer. "It'll last for a hundred years," he thinks. But the wooden tank that holds the Paris green solution is another matter. Rough and weather-beaten, it looks its age.

Applying Paris green is a nasty business. Pete sits on the sprayer and drives the horse while two of his sons walk behind and direct the hoses at the lush green plants. Insecticide issues forth. Although its chief target is the plants, the spray coats everything in close proximity. Before the field is finished, the boys' arms, hands, and legs from the knees down are bright green. They're soaked with spray. It even infiltrates their nostrils; they sneeze Paris green into their handkerchiefs. Their mother won't let the arsenic-laden boys into the house: much too messy. "Go back outside and wash at the pump," she orders, shooing them away with her hand and sweeping the porch after them.

In 1911, when North Branchers are pursuing summer activities—fishing outings to Sunrise Lake, band concerts in the evenings, baseball games with Pine City or Taylors Falls—the potato market opens unusually early, on July 13. Because of the dry winter and early spring, some farmers got their seed in early, in April, as Pete did, and the small, tender-skinned new potatoes are ready for market. The farmers who planted early are reaping the benefits: merchants in town will pay $1.25 for each bushel of new potatoes, a whopping good price. Most of Pete's potatoes aren't anywhere near ready, but this early market activity is promising. In the next few weeks, as he cuts and threshes his rye crop and makes hay under the blazing heat of a July sun, Pete thinks about the possibilities contained within a hefty potato check. A new barn, perhaps? Or maybe a piano? Some of his neighbors have caught the automobile bug and come home with a shiny new Imperial or Overland. But he'd really have no use for an auto. A farmer doesn't have time to go out on Sunday afternoon drives.

The great wheel of the seasons has turned, and the constellation of Orion rises in the night sky. Sumac flames on the edges of wood lots, and the bur oaks, though still green, appear dusty and faded. Russet-colored prairie grasses fringe the cultivated fields. The small grains—rye, oats—have been cut and threshed, sacked and stored, the fields in which they grew reduced to stubble. The potato vines have withered and faded to the color of straw. Their wispy remains mark the hills under which hide the tubers that will keep Pete Swanson's farm solvent for another year.

There is an expectancy to the September air: cooler nights, then a frost. Finally, in November, the first lasting snow plunges the land into dormancy. But that is not the whole of it. An anticipation rests on the town, on the farms, this year: the outlook for potatoes in the fall of 1911 is extremely bright. Agricultural experts predict a record crop of twenty million bushels, the largest potato harvest ever produced in Minnesota. Nine buyers of potato wholesale firms have already set up shop in North Branch, and they figure that the North Branch region alone will produce half a million bushels.

By 1911 very few potato farmers dig by hand anymore. In North Branch, Oleson and Bergwell Implements, representatives of OK Champion Diggers, have sold carloads of diggers in the past few years, but Pete owns a Dowden, bought from Splittstoser, which he feels is more effective at unearthing all the potatoes clustered in a hill. Diggers require a lot of horsepower. Some brands, in fact, are considered "horse killers" for the demand they make on the animals that pull them. Pete selects four of his biggest horses for the arduous work of dragging the Dowden through the soil. Sandy soil actually makes the task more difficult, since both the horses' hooves and the wheels of the digger sink deeper than they would on clay. The horses will work a long day in the field, straining slowly down the rows, bringing potatoes to the surface.

The digger only does so much of the work, though. Once the potatoes are unearthed and lie pale and exposed on the soil, human hands need to collect them into bushel baskets and prepare them for storage. On Pete's farm, this backbreaking work is done by the children, who are released from school for two weeks each fall for a "potato vacation." This is a "perk" garnered mainly by farm children. The school in town tolerates, but does not encourage, absence from school for fieldwork, but many country schools in Chisago County actually establish two-week leaves in contracts with their schoolteachers.

One might think the children would be gleeful, released from school for these weeks when the trees are turning and the weather is warm, but they have mixed feelings about the vacation. It is fun to be away from school, but the work is so demanding and seemingly unending that even their young backs ache and complain under the exertion. The dry taupe sand grinds into every fold and wrinkle of their hands and feet, as the barefoot children creep down the rows picking up tubers and putting them in bushel baskets. A horse-drawn "scoot," holding about ten baskets, hauls the potatoes to a central location in the field. They are piled into immense mounds, creamy piles of Kennebecs and rosy heaps of red-skinned Ohios. These mounds, called "pits," will be covered by straw or hay and a little soil to protect them from frost. A circle on the ground keeps count of how many bushels are in each pit. Every time a bushel is dumped, one potato is thrown into the circle.

Pete never actually pays his children for their work at harvest-time: it's considered part of their responsibility to the family. However, on a Saturday night trip into town there might be a little pocket money handed out for the spending.

The Swansons work with single-minded purpose during the potato harvest, hoping that rain or extreme cold won't set in and impede their efforts. A ferocious cold spell can freeze potatoes yet undug, rendering them useless and biting into profits. While the good weather holds, Pete has time for little else than eating, sleeping, chores, and digging. Once the potatoes are all pitted, he will take the time to move them from the pit into his root cellar or to load and haul them to town for shipping.

Even in the best economic times, the potato market is volatile, prices remaining steady for weeks, then plunging without warning; it is a tough call for farmers on whether to sell in the fall or to store the potatoes and sell in the winter. Freak weather, foreign production, consumer demand in the South—so many aspects factor into the price that potato growing is dicey, any way you cut it. Pete usually hedges his bets and does a little of both: he'll sell some spuds in October and November and hold some back, hoping the price will rise toward spring.

Not all of Pete's potatoes are destined for the dinner table. As he sacks his potatoes, he separates the smallest ones that can't be sold on the market, loads them into the wagon, and takes them into one of the starch factories in town. There, these "culls" will be ground into bits, dried, and pulverized to form potato starch. There is a narrow window of opportunity to sell to a starch factory. They open in late September for only a few weeks, so if he wants to make money on the culls, Pete needs to get them into town promptly.

Despite the numerous carloads of potatoes heading out of town by rail, life is lively at the starch factory this fall. As Pete's weathered wagon, brimming with runty potatoes, creaks into town, he notices that there'll be a wait at the starch factory today. Off to the north of downtown, a line of wagons curls down First Street, the patient horses drooped and dozing. A factory employee will weigh each load one by one, then direct it to the large chute where the culls will be dumped into the factory. The mammoth graters, consuming the culls, whine in the background as the waiting farmers greet each other, light pipes, and settle in for the duration.

As repositories for otherwise worthless potatoes, the starch factories are priceless institutions in North Branch. In poor potato years, when the bulk of tubers are small, scabby, or both, farmers can sell to the factories and earn some money on their crop. Not enough to make them rich, but enough to keep their families fed and clothed. The starch, produced by the ton, is not for consumption. The Farmers' Starch Factory ships it out to textile- and paper-producing centers, to stiffen fabric and paper. For years, starch manufacturing has been big business. Daily consumption in the United States is estimated at thousands of tons.

The 1911 potato harvest does not disappoint the buyers or the farmers, who report record yields, as high as four hundred bushels per acre. Despite the overproduction, prices remain favorable all fall. When Pete hauls in a wagonload of Triumphs in early November, he gets seventy cents for each bushel. At sixty bushels per load, that's forty-two dollars for a single load, approximately the cost of four winter overcoats at Edelstein's Dry Goods.

In January 1912, the *North Branch Review* publishes the railroad station's statistics on potato shipments from August through the first week in January: 402 carloads (worth $140,000) of potatoes have left town by rail, with perhaps as many still stored in the town's twelve warehouses. The total valuation of potatoes for the 1911 season is estimated at just under three hundred thousand dollars. At the end of the century, in Pete's grandson Doug's time, the value of those spuds would equal six million dollars.

Late in January, a thaw sets in after what has been a horrifically cold winter. Lake Superior has frozen over, a rare event, and in midmonth the nearby community of Harris records a nighttime temperature of negative fifty degrees Fahrenheit. There have been reports that some farmers' stored potatoes have frozen in their root cellars, a blow to future profits. With the break in the cold, Pete decides that it is time to get his stored potatoes to market. The snow is packed, the roads are good for sleighing, and prices have been pleasantly high. Back and forth he goes, hauling sack after sack of Kennebecs up the root cellar steps, into the wintry outdoors, and on to the waiting sled. The potatoes have declined very little in quality—still firm, unsprouted, with the last grains of soil clinging to their pale, creamy skins.

A January thaw is not necessarily mild, especially in a cold winter. It only feels balmy. Pete is swathed in woolen outer garments on the short trip to town, a sleighload of spuds for ballast behind him. The horses' heads are wreathed in frosty breath as they leave the farmyard at a trot. The oak wood lots are deep in drifts. The sleigh bells chime cheerily over the snowy landscape.

For Pete, this is the social event of the fortnight, an opportunity to smoke a few pipes, swap a few stories, catch up on the news. He is a strict teetotaler, in keeping with church teaching, but others might once have stopped in at Frank Olson's for a few beers. Alas, by 1912 the temperance movement has swept through North Branch, and the saloon was closed three years ago.

The trip home is quicker without the potatoes, and the team enters the farmyard just as the setting sun casts its rosy rays over the deepening blue of the snowy fields. It is time for supper and chores.

The End of an Era

AT FIRST GLANCE, North Branch has little to recommend it. It is not pretty, nor distinctive. "Plain as a mud fence," Tom would remark as we'd drive into town after a vacation, cross the one intersection controlled by a stoplight, and gaze about the modest two-block business district with fresh eyes. The silvery storage elevators of Peterson's Mill and the slender spire of the old Swedish Lutheran church are the chief structural elements in the skyline. The one-story storefronts are squat and downright.homely. When we lived in town, city hall was an unremarkable prefabricated structure adjacent to the municipal liquor store. Grace and artistry, it appears, do not reside here.

When we moved to town in 1984, it seemed pinched in other ways as well. The old school, then serving as the middle school, had been added on to so many times that it resembled a mishmash of building blocks. One of the additions included an auditorium that served as the only community gathering space, although it was too small, its seating battered and worn. The community had steadfastly refused to build either a swimming pool or a fine arts performance auditorium for the high school, labeling both as frills. And, the town had never had a vital, well-stocked library.

After years spent in the elegant river town of St. Peter, Minnesota, and in the Lake Superior community of Ashland, Wisconsin, we often wondered how we had come to settle in such a nondescript town. The tales our older neighbors told of the great potato era intrigued me because it seemed a prestigious—well, at least a prosperous—past had left no legacy to the town. Great bounty seemed at odds with the meager life the town now led. Where had it all gone?

I asked the older people when and why the potato industry died out and received vague and varied replies. Most cited as an endpoint and cause the onset of the Great Depression, but none are historians. No one has a broad overview of the three or four decades when North Branch was hailed as the hub of the Potato Belt. Even the oldest people, those in their nineties, were only small children in 1911, when production was at its peak. They remember their parents' stories but have no personal memories of the thousand carloads of potatoes leaving the North Branch station each year.

"Why did farmers stop growing potatoes?" I asked my seasoned quartet of potato experts, farmers in their seventies to nineties who farmed sand land outside of Harris, north of North Branch.

"Disease," said Tom Johnson promptly.

"Seed stock ran out," added Fillmore Johnson.

Roy Hammerstrom had the longest answer. "When farmers grew alfalfa for dairy cows, they had to lime the soil—alfalfa likes alkaline soil. But then that field was no good for potatoes." Soft-spoken Allan Jarchow nodded in agreement.

I would find that each of them had part of the answer.

The history of the potato industry on the Anoka Sand Plain is not detailed in the classic works on Minnesota history. Instead, historians of that time period focus on the more dramatic ways the state's citizens exploited the land's wealth of natural resources. Accounts of the state's early twentieth century describe the iron ore industry on the Mesabi Range and the logging of the last white pine forests. Because of the paucity of scholarly attention, much of what I know about Potato City, its rise and fall, has been gleaned from hours spent in the gray light of the Minnesota Historical Society's library, fingering the yellowed pages of old agricultural bulletins, flipping through weekly issues of the *Potato Digest* (a fitting name), and scrolling through illuminated microfilm copies of the town's weekly newspaper, the *North Branch Review*. The newspaper has been the most revealing source.

One drawback of depending on newspapers to explain history is that the window into the past is only as big as the editor chose to make it. The first editor of the *Review*, John Huber, chronicled the birth of the potato industry. Huber cofounded the newspaper in 1891 and presided over it for the next fourteen years. Witty and humorous, feisty in editorial battle, Huber was the one to bestow on North Branch its nickname: "Potato City"—or, if he was in a by-jingo mood, "Pot-8-O City." Editor Huber took a keen interest in the town's main industry and filled his newspaper's pages with lively reports of the potato market, the goings-on at the two starch factories, and the effect of the weather on the crop.

In the era before county extension agents and widespread agricultural research, Huber's erudition served as a source of information for the farming community. When an outbreak of "worms" moved through east-central Minnesota in June 1898, defoliating trees and festooning branches with gauzy, beige cocoons, it was editor Huber, wielding his "T" encyclopedia, who identified them as tent caterpillars. A fundamental knowledge of natural history was lacking because few farmers had long-term experience on the sand plain. In the 1890s, only a handful of adults were native to the area; a sizeable percentage was most conversant with Swedish soil. Not many knew this particular patch of earth well.

Although John Huber was a classic booster, eager to extol the

North Branch community as a paragon, it was he who first intimated to his readers—and to me, perusing his newspaper a century later—that something was amiss in the Eden of the sand plain. Early in 1894, the *Review* noted the occurrence of scab on the previous year's crop. This comment was followed two months later by an editorial observing that farmers would soon need to fertilize their fields if they wished to maintain the yields of the past decade. Then, in April 1894, Huber ran an article on blight and rot, two diseases that had followed potato farmers from the Old World to the new.

By 1894, area farmers had been producing potatoes for about ten years. The opening of Reuel Hall's starch factory in 1889 marked the beginning of a large-scale potato industry, but the factory's second owner, Mr. S. H. Hall, observed several years later in the pages of the *Review* that farmers had raised some potatoes before the starch factory was built. Ten years is all it took for the diseases that had plagued European potato farmers for centuries to reach the Minnesota sand lands, threatening to transform the early years of potato farming into a paradise lost.

In 1900, Huber wrote an editorial column urging farmers to buy seed stock from outside the state. Minnesota seed stock, it seemed, had "run back" and "lost its identity"—vague, nonscientific phrases indicating that the seed was not producing desirable tubers. Here was another potentially alarming circumstance. North Branch not only produced potatoes for the table but also had an established industry raising seed stock for southern states, which could not store their own seed through their warm winters. (Potato growers—then and now—do not use seeds, that is, ovules, to grow a new crop. They cut tubers grown the previous season, termed "seeds" or "seed stock," which generate vegetatively.) A problem with the seed potatoes was a worrisome situation indeed.

Throughout the rest of his tenure at the *Review*, Huber ran periodic articles on potato disease and recorded the twists and turns of the ever-volatile market. He called for multiple-crop farming, arguing that farmers shouldn't be dependent on a cash crop so much at the mercy of disease and an unpredictable market. He also advocated the establishment of a creamery, which would bring dairy farming into the region, giving farmers another way to make a living off the land.

All the reasons mentioned by my quartet of potato farmers had appeared in the *Review* before John Huber sold it in 1905. Yet at that time the industry did not seem affected by these afflictions. It grew and grew. Warehouses to store the bumper crops blossomed alongside the railroad track. The potato starch factories turned out thousands of tons of starch. Splittstoser Manufacturing, based in North Branch, reorganized and bought out a Kansas firm, expanding to produce potato farming implements that were shipped all over the United States and Canada. In 1911, with an estimated two million bushels of potatoes marketed, Chisago County's crop was valued at one and a half million dollars. "Hurrah for old Chisago County!" the *Review*'s editor exulted, "and her ever reliable crop of 'spuds.'"

Black leg. Scab. Dry rot. Blight. Black rot. Leaf spot. Black scurf. The names slither like toads and snakes off the lips of the speaker.

What these diseases do to a potato plant is even less appealing. Black leg, a bacterial disease flourishing in wet seasons, begins underground and advances upward, the stems turning slimy and inky black. Scab is a fungal disease that affects the tuber's skin. Surface lesions form, rendering the potato undesirable for table use. Early blight, a.k.a. leaf spot, is also fungal. The leaves turn yellow and die; the tubers are runty and unmarketable. Late blight, historically the most infamous of the diseases, was responsible for the starvation deaths of over one and a half million Irish in the Great Potato Famine of 1846. Also a fungal disease, late blight begins as a white fuzzy ring on the undersurface of a leaf. As the fungus spreads, it attacks the stems, then the tubers, which subsequently rot in storage. It may produce a fetid, characteristic odor. Old-time growers claimed they could smell blight hanging over a field.

For the North Branch farmers, perhaps the most distressing of the diseases was dry rot, because it only manifested itself under the right conditions. A field of seemingly healthy plants might produce a good yield of apparently sound tubers that filled with black or brown rotted tissue in storage. Seed infected with the fungus might not produce noticeably diseased plants for several years, if growing conditions did not favor the fungus's spread. But once established in a region, the fungus had great staying power. It existed in the soil for years, and it transferred to the inside walls of root cellars and warehouses, contaminating them as well.

All of these diseases lodged in the once-pristine virgin soil. Infected seed, wilted leaves, and rotting tubers could all play host to a large number of pathogens. Small, scabby potatoes whose flesh was sound were frequently cooked and fed to livestock—pigs and cows. But if their manure was then spread on fields, those fields, too, harbored the fungus. Like smallpox, Norway rats, and the European immigrants themselves, the potato plant's pathogens found an open, hospitable environment to exploit in the New World.

Farmers were not completely defenseless against these diseases, and the arsenal available to them was strikingly similar to that enjoyed by their counterparts today. They were admonished by experts from University Farm (the agricultural arm of the University of Minnesota, residing on today's St. Paul campus) to use vigorous seed and disinfect it by dipping it in fungicide; to rotate crops, growing potatoes in the same field only every fourth year; to select varieties resistant to certain diseases; and to spray with a solution known as "Bordeaux mixture," a concoction of copper sulfate and lime.

A fifth suggestion was unique to the age. It was to use "new soil"—virgin soil, soil free from the diseases of agriculture—for a potato crop. And that is what North Branch farmers were able to do for a number of years into the twentieth century. They cleared their remaining wild land, the oak savanna, acre by acre, moving their fields farther and farther out. When there was no more oak savanna left, this option closed to them. The Review alluded tangentially to its passing in 1913, noting that the area's supply of wood for home heating was gone and soon residents would need to employ coal.

The use of chemical compounds to combat disease—then and now—is a mixed blessing. The anti-fungal dipping solution for seed potatoes was corrosive sublimate, also known as mercuric chloride, a cumulative poison that collects in living tissue over the years. Mercury exposure can cause insanity: *Alice in Wonderland*'s Mad Hatter had used mercuric compounds in crafting his hats.

Bordeaux mixture could be combined with the arsenic-based Paris green, another poison and a known carcinogen. As any reader of murder mysteries knows, arsenic poisoning is an effective and subtle way to bump off an annoying character. (This fact wasn't lost on early North Branchers. The *Review*'s pages contain several accounts of suicides brought about by ingestion of Paris green. It wasn't a pleasant way to go, though. Victims usually lingered several agonizing days before succumbing to the poison.) These poisonous compounds, even when used "properly," ended up in the soil and in the waterways of the sand plain.

Applied simultaneously, the deadly Bordeaux/Paris green brew saved the farmer some work, but as researchers gained more experience with the diseases and the fungicides that controlled them, they found that farmers needed a high-pressure sprayer—an additional expense—to render the Bordeaux mixture truly effective. Most farmers had invested in a low-pressure sprayer to disseminate Paris green, when the potatoes' only enemy was the potato bug. It must have gone against the thrifty Swedes' principles to have to replace a perfectly functional low-pressure sprayer.

But it was an expense that needed to be incorporated into the ledger of every grower if farmers were serious about potato farming. On the pages of the *North Branch Review* appeared frequent warnings from plant pathologists at University Farm, like this one from April 1913, only two years after the record two-million-bushel potato crop: "Diseases, particularly those of the soil, are commencing to gain a foothold in this state.... Do not wait until the diseases are so bad that Minnesota seed potatoes are always suspected of disease.... Diseases [will] gradually increase until the land is practically worthless for potatoes."

The production of attractive, healthy potatoes for the dining table was one thing. If the tubers looked good and kept well in storage, wholesalers would buy them. The production of seed potatoes destined to generate the next season's crop was another. Since diseases could lurk undetected, producers needed to offer some sort of guarantee that their seed was "clean." By the late 1910s, the university researchers' predictions had come true: Minnesota-grown seed potatoes had developed a bad reputation among southern potato growers. In 1922, the *Potato Digest* printed a crushing assessment of the seed potato industry: "The name 'Minnesota' has become a trade name for scrap stuff and it is applied to poor stock from any state."

Latent bacterial and fungal diseases were not the only plagues on seed potatoes. An additional problem mystified potato growers. North Branch farmers noticed that their seed potatoes degenerated after many years of vegetative propagation. The farmers called it "running out" or "running back." Plants grown from last year's cut-up tubers lost their vigor and produced runty, misshapen tubers. They "lost their identity." Much later, plant pathologists would discover that this mysterious phenomenon was due to viruses that accumulated in seed stock and were passed along season after season. The virus's genetic material incorporated itself into the plant's DNA; tubers harboring a virus in their cells were used as seeds, which then grew another plant also infected with the virus. Had potatoes reproduced sexually, with ovum and pollen, like most crops, viruses would not have carried over to the next year's crop or accumulated over the years.

One way to ward off an accumulation of viral diseases was by setting up seed plots so that production of new seed potatoes could be diligently overseen. When viral diseases expressed themselves in a plant, that plant and its tubers would be destroyed or "rogued out." But in the years before the nature of viruses was understood, they were harder to curb than fungal or bacterial disease.

In letters to the *Potato Digest*, southern buyers alternately berated Minnesota growers for their poor seed and encouraged them to certify that their seed was disease-free. In response to the decline in quality, the State of Minnesota, the university, and the Minnesota Potato Exchange, a potato growers' cooperative, joined forces to inspect and certify seed potatoes.

The process to become certified was necessarily rigorous. Farmers applying for certification needed to maintain a seed plot, a small portion of field set aside to grow their own source of seed. The seed plot was carefully monitored, inspected, and certified, and fields required two inspections before being pronounced "clean." Annual potato tours of certain farms were set up to show prospective buyers the field conditions under which the seed stock was grown. Potato farming was becoming a science, a far cry from the "plant 'em and dig 'em" early days, and the *Digest* noted, "only the most progressive farmers, those willing to become thoroughly acquainted with the problems involved in the production of good seed potatoes" would have their potatoes inspected.

In 1917, the first year of certification, only three North Branch farmers had fields that met the criteria. A year later, several growers from the sand plain community of Isanti became certified. The vast majority of certified seed potato producers were from northern Minnesota, and that region maintained its dominance in the coming decade. Despite the demand for disease-free seed from potato brokers in the South, and the fact that certified potatoes turned a profit for farmers even in poor growing years, farmers didn't welcome the yoke of certification. A Maine plant pathologist involved in certification noted, "Our efforts 'to help the farmer' are not always appreciated, and this is no exception to the rule." Unable to meet the rigorous standards, the seed potato industry dwindled from the sand plain.

In 1895, a full decade before potatoes became big business in North Branch, editor Huber reported in the *Review* that farmers west of town were calling for a creamery. Their appeal came in the middle of the potato harvest, a year in which a plethora of potatoes glutted the market and caused prices to plummet. Casting about for other ways to make a living off the sand plain, the community searched for one that offered stability to farmers and to the North Branch businesses that relied on them for an economic base. The boom and bust nature of the volatile potato market gave farmers the sense of that new-fangled amusement, the roller coaster ride.

Dairy farming offered the desired stability. Cows produced milk daily, so checks from the creamery provided constant income to the farmer. The practice of raising several different crops as fodder for the cows gave the industry less absolute dependence on the vagaries of the weather. But unlike potato farming, dairying could not be done independently. First, farmers needed a nearby outlet for their highly perishable milk. The rapidly expanding Twin Cities beckoned as a potential market for milk producers in east-central Minnesota. Second, creameries were needed to process the milk. These creameries required a certain number of cows to operate profitably, meaning that many farmers had to commit to dairying before a creamery could be built.

Despite its size and prominence in Chisago County, North Branch was one of the last towns on the eastern edge of the sand plain to build a creamery. The much smaller communities of Almelund, Kost, and Spring Lake all had well-established creameries before the North Branch Creamery opened in May 1910 with six hundred cows supporting it. The creamery initially produced butter; later it also accepted milk, which was pasteurized, bottled, and shipped to the Cities.

Dairy farming involved a learning curve. A key crop to promote the health and vigor of dairy cows was alfalfa. By 1920, Chisago County's first agricultural agent, Carl Morck, had arrived to advise area farmers. Mr. Morck used his expertise and position to nudge farmers into alfalfa production as an alternative to the wiregrass hay traditionally used as fodder for milk cows. Alfalfa-fed cows grew bigger and produced more milk than those skimping along on wiregrass. But the first attempts to grow alfalfa on the sand foundered. Fields were sparse; plants spindly. The sand, slightly acidic, lacked the calcium needed for lush growth. Agent Morck set up demonstration fields to showcase what adding lime to the soil could do for the alfalfa crop. The results, documented by photos, were convincing.

But potatoes flourish in acidic soil. The farmer who limed his fields turned his back on potato production. The year 1920 was decisive for potatoes and for dairy cows. In that year, two railroad cars carrying crushed limestone rolled into town, and thus began an attempt to change the fundamental nature of the sand. Farmers applied lime at a rate of two tons per acre, and the pH of the soil became basic (alkaline). Agricultural data from the 1920s reveal exponential growth in alfalfa acreage. Agent Morck reported to the *Potato Digest* in 1922 that "while the crop looked good in [his] neck of the woods . . . potato acreage had decreased by 20% from previous years."

Still, I wanted confirmation of my pieced-together history. I longed for certainty, for someone to rise from the dusty pages in the library and announce, "It's over. The first giddy wave of potato farming has foundered on the realities of disease." Then one day I came across a brief comment tucked into a back page of a *Potato Digest* issue from 1922, a paragraph so small that its message must have been common knowledge. "North Branch," the *Digest* observed,

> was at one time considered the hub of the potato industry and perhaps it is the center of early activities along the line of real commercial production, being one of the heaviest shippers, if not the heaviest. Sixteen to twenty years ago, it sometimes shipped as high as 1,200 carloads for a season, but this year about 75 to 100 carloads is the limit.

Here was my answer: North Branch was the cradle that launched the industry, but by 1922 its time had passed.

Potato farming didn't end abruptly. A 1937 report on the potato industry in Minnesota noted that total acreage devoted to potato production in the sand lands reached a maximum in 1931 but that the yield per acre was half that of 1925. In North Branch, the Farmers' Starch Factory sold out in 1924 and converted to a pickle factory. Splittstoser Implement Company closed its doors a few years later, a victim of the Great Depression. After the wave had crested, it slowly receded, leaving behind only sand.

Oak Hill Cemetery

FALL DESCENDS UPON MINNESOTA, bringing golden days in which the land seems lit from within. A glow illumines the air, appearing to originate not from an external sun but out of the grass and trees themselves, warm with color and suppressed life. People who live in northern climates cherish these days, for though the golden languor hints at timelessness, we know the hourglass is running out. Winter will soon follow.

On such a day I wandered up to Oak Hill Cemetery in North Branch, on the high southern bank of the Sunrise River. Inexplicably, in fifteen years of living in town I had never visited this cemetery. Our family had been many times to the Lutheran cemetery, also on the riverbank, a hundred yards away. When our children were learning to ride bicycles, that cemetery had been a favorite destination on trips about town. On the graveyard's empty paved roads, the kids had been free to take spills and wobble about on their two-wheelers without serious consequences. But Oak Hill's paths are gravel and it is tucked farther back, beyond the west-side neighborhood, so we never visited.

It was a pity I had waited so long. Oak Hill was a lovely place, especially in the topaz light of the late fall afternoon. Situated on a gentle rise of land—a "hill" only in the North Branch sense—the cemetery was graced with many large, twisted bur oaks, bereft of leaves, appearing now, in November, at once contorted and serene. The north branch of the Sunrise River wound around the cemetery's northern perimeter, its waters having cut a deep bank through the sand plain. The river itself was not visible, but on the edge of the cemetery grew clusters of red oaks, their dry leaves rustling softly with every breath of air.

Oak Hill harbored many old grave markers, proportionately more, it seemed, than did the Lutheran cemetery. This was in keeping with the pattern of settlement: the Swedish Lutherans had organized their congregation thirty years after the Yankees had first settled in the area, to live and die on the sand plain.

I had come to Oak Hill to look for two of those early pioneers: Dr. Thomas Zeien and his wife, Mary. Born in North Washington, Iowa, to German immigrants, Dr. Zeien had arrived in east-central Minnesota fresh from medical school in the mid-1880s and remained in the area all his life. He had married a schoolteacher from nearby Rock Creek, Mary Redoute, and they had raised three children. He retired in 1933, after forty years of doctoring the people of North Branch. After such a long practice he probably had remained in town, and I knew of no other possible cemeteries. Oak Hill was a logical place to look.

As the Doctor's Wife, I felt an affinity with the Zeiens. Much of what I'd garnered of their lives seemed true of ours also. Despite advanced medical technology and "wonder drugs," we had emergency calls in the middle of the night, dinners interrupted and plans disrupted by sick people needing a doctor. Dr. Zeien frequently gazed on bloody injuries, wondering what needed to be done. Mary often had sole care of those three young children. I could relate.

My interest in locating their graves was more difficult to explain. Superficially, I suppose, it was a quest, a lighthearted excuse to stroll through an old cemetery on a sunny afternoon. But probing deeper, I realized that I desired to make them real. With only brief newspaper stories and snatches of old people's memories to bring him to life, Dr. Zeien was something of a shade to me, Mrs. Zeien even shadier. I wanted to know what remained after one raised children, worked hard, was a good neighbor, and poured one's lifeblood into a community. Did anything linger? Was it possible to disappear without a trace?

I have always been attracted to old cemeteries. This is far from a morbid fascination: I find graveyards to be small oases of serenity. It is reassuring that, despite the tempests of daily life—the frantic search for enough time, the difficulties infusing all relationships, the passions that swell and ebb in the heart—one will eventually reach a safe harbor, and that harbor will be a cemetery, quiet, calm, and peaceful.

This attraction first manifested itself in a college sociology project, when a friend and I surveyed epitaphs on gravestones in St. Peter, one of the earliest towns to be settled in Minnesota. The project gathered an odd assortment of posthumous commentary. The blandest, of course, were the Bible verses. My favorite was a four-line poem, repeated in a number of variations, which I read each time with a pleasant shiver:

> Remember, Friend, as you pass by
> As you are now, so once was I.
> As I am now, so shall you be.
> Prepare for Death and follow me.

What I came to realize early on, and what still interests me, is that history is laid bare on the markers of a cemetery, but not in a straightforward way. It requires detective work, using clues and tidbits of disorganized information to piece together the stories of human lives, the remains of which lie six feet below. With a little effort these narratives spring to life: a diphtheria epidemic that takes a disproportionate number of children during one winter, a woman's early death in childbirth, her baby dying soon after. Sad stories in some cases; tales of a long life in others.

I had been indulging myself in old cemeteries this first week in November: Oak Hill was the third cemetery I'd visited in six days. (It seemed an excessive amount, even to me. Much as I enjoy them, cemetery visits are often punctuated by years rather than days.)

The week had begun with the church feast of All Saints' Day, a celebration of the dead. I like this Christian festival. I like its rousing signature hymn, "For All the Saints," and the candles that flicker on the white-clothed altar, one for each life of the congregation's recently deceased. But my visits to the cemeteries were not conscious commemorations of saints. In fact, they were not planned in any way. I had visited the first, a tiny graveyard attached to an equally small Lutheran church in rural Isanti County, to pass the time while my child took a music lesson.

I had visited the second to ferret out part of my family's past. My seventy-three-year-old mother, the last of her generation, and I had poked about in St. Paul's large and sprawling Oakland Cemetery to uncover the earliest graves of the Moeller family, our immigrant ancestors who had come to St. Paul in the 1850s. I wanted my mother to point out their location while she was still alert and active. I wanted to stand with her on the hill overlooking Minnesota's capitol building, where, underneath an ancient bur oak, lay our link to Germany and our earliest tie to the New World.

All three cemeteries had two characteristics in common: each had been carved out of wild oak savanna, retaining the red and bur oaks, now large and impressive, to shade the present and future graves, and each harbored what we in Minnesota consider to be "old graves."

Both of these features bear pondering. By sheltering within their confines the last of the savanna oaks, the cemeteries are the graveyards not only of the state's pioneers but also of the savanna itself. They hold the remains of the original ecosystem. I imagined the pioneers selecting a parcel of wild land, perhaps for its proximity to a church yard or a river or, in the case of Oakland Cemetery, for its panoramic view of town, cordoning it off and setting it aside as an untouched place in which to bury their dead. All around, trees are cut, sod is plowed, and humanity presses onward, gobbling up the wilderness, but the cemetery becomes a time capsule, removed from the pursuit of Progress. It is an unwitting and oddly natural way to preserve components of the ecosystem.

The fact that we consider the graves in these three cemeteries to be "old" underscores the callow youth of Minnesota. Only in North America, only in the western half of the continent, could 130-year-old graves be considered "old." I can trace my family back only four generations, to those graves under the bur oak in Oakland Cemetery. Earlier than that yawns the chasm of Europe, a dark, featureless unknown that because of war, the Black Plague, and the passage of time will remain unknowable. Even some of the oaks have lived on this savanna soil longer than our tenure here.

Now in North Branch's Oak Hill Cemetery and gazing about, I noted that it was not very large. It would take me perhaps an hour to survey the place, a pleasant hour spent meandering between headstones, scuffing up oak leaves, sniffing their dry sweetness of decay, and enjoying the crunch as they crumpled underfoot. The November afternoon was unusually warm; the temperature had risen to a record seventy-seven degrees the day before. I shrugged off my jacket and left it in the car as I took up my clipboard and headed toward the nearest marker.

The first markers I inspected were very old and rough to the touch. The once-smooth granite and marble slabs had been pitted by wind-borne sand, which scoured clean the facts of existence. This gentle but ceaseless erosion made it impossible to identify names and dates. Even though I tried, my fingers carefully tracing the carved indentations, I could not decipher the letters. The sand would conquer completely. Not content to claim the physical remains of the former North Branch residents, it was also rasping away these monuments to their lives.

It was frustrating to be unable to read the headstones. I couldn't recall having had that problem before, at least not in Minnesota. I wondered if sand was noticeably more abrasive than other soil types. Or perhaps it was merely that a full quarter-century had passed since I had studied headstones in earnest and, consequently, the oldest stones were just that much more illegible.

I moved on to a nearby obelisk that was slender and graceful in scale, nearly as tall as me. This one I deciphered. It was Judge Ephraim Ingalls and his wife, Cordelia. The judge had died in February 1895, according to the *Review*. One week, the paper noted he was ill; the next week, he was dead. The issue carrying his official obituary was missing, however. Perhaps his passing had been momentous enough that someone had cut it out or tucked the paper away, so that the library would not, in the future, have a complete collection of *North Branch Reviews*.

Originally hailing from Sunrise City, twelve miles east of North Branch, the judge was the son of early Chisago County pioneers. Active in Republican politics at a time when most of the town voted Republican, he was a venerated leader. One gets the impression that he was the steadying hand in a newly formed town bustling with young people. Wide of girth (a newspaper account estimated it at sixty inches when a pair of his pants appeared as part of a prankster's costume in a Fourth of July parade), with a genial nature, the judge was highly regarded for his shrewd assessment of human nature, whether in the courtroom or in the political arena.

My mind's eye called up images of black-garbed figures knotted around an open grave on a cold February day, the sky bright blue, the north wind sharp, the human beings bereft with the sense that with his death an age had passed into history.

Judge Ingalls and Cordelia lie apart from the other headstones, as if they belong to a now-distant past. I walked west, toward the newer part of the cemetery. In this section, the graves were tended. Plastic flowers clung to some stones; zinnias and marigolds, blackened by frost, adorned others. Though a number of graves were recent, I did not recognize most of the names, a stark contrast to my visits to the Lutheran cemetery, where faces and names and stories shape themselves all around me. Although he often exaggerates certain features of life in a rural community, Garrison Keillor accurately assesses a small town's segregation by religion. My husband and I ran with a mostly Lutheran crowd. In fact, during our first four years in North Branch, before our oldest child entered the public school, we could count on one hand the number of non-Lutheran friends we had. That had changed as we met other parents through school activities, but now I saw, in the two cemeteries adjacent to each other, that ecumenical mixing remained transitory.

In the next section of Oak Hill, large, imposing double headstones—not obelisks, not flat head markers—were in vogue. My interest quickened as I recognized the names on them. Bergh! He owned the Scandinavian Drugstore, the one on Main Street that sold Paris green at the best price in town. Two babies, their deaths a year apart, were also buried near the Scandinavian druggist. The newspaper accounts that had provided me with a glimpse into North Branch life of the 1890s didn't begin to reveal the heartache—or, probably, the happy times—that had once filled these human lives.

"Carter," I read. Wallace Carter had owned the town's meat market. "For a nice, tender steak, go to Carter's" the ad in the *Review* advised. Wallace's oldest son had died of typhoid fever in Superior, Wisconsin, at age nineteen. I noted his flat headstone off to one side. He was stricken in 1894, the same year as the great Hinckley fire. The two Carter parents had taken a train to Superior to be with Len as he lay ill, passing through the scorched remains of Hinckley only two months after the devastating conflagration.

Emil Brandes was lining the outer edge of the cemetery. Arriving from St. Paul to temporarily manage North Branch's lumber-yard, this thirty-something bachelor stayed on to become a potato buyer for C. A. Bugge. The newspaper reported him building a house in town in August 1893, then settling down in earnest with a bride from Kenyon, Minnesota, one month later. The paper's society column had ribbed him about his matrimonial adventure—I presumed, reading between the lines, because he had been a hardened bachelor, smitten at last by a young woman eleven years his junior.

The Locke family plot was nearby. John Locke had lost a new house to fire in the summer of a drought year. He had not had insurance and the loss was staggering—$1,200—but a man needs a house and he rebuilt immediately.

I smiled when I saw John Huber's headstone. Here was the first editor of the *North Branch Review*. Having filled the pages of his newspaper with wry, acerbic wit, Huber became a primary source for what I've learned of the town's history. What he deemed of interest, he put into his weekly editions. Gleaning his bits and pieces, I was able to reconstruct the life and commerce of our town. I owe—all of us owe—a great deal to John Huber, I thought, as I patted his headstone.

And then, at last, lying close to his friend was Dr. Zeien, and his wife, Mary. Their double headstone was engraved with a border of intertwining oak leaves. Perhaps they had cherished North Branch's oaks as I do. Their daughter, Rosalie, born (I noted) on the same date as my daughter and never married, was buried in the same plot. She, I remembered, was the child who accidentally ate the bread crust laced with rat poison and survived to become the woman who was a legendary teacher in North Branch High School, the gray-haired librarian that my contemporaries in town remember from their childhood.

"So you are real," I mentally addressed the doctor's headstone. "Of all the people here, you probably knew more of the town's secrets than anyone else. Doctors always do. And you probably harbored secrets about yourself, as well—the panic you experienced when you were called to a serious farm accident and realized that medical school had never prepared you for that kind of mess; the frustration of not being able to diagnose a baffling set of symptoms and watching helplessly as your patient, most likely a friend or neighbor, slipped away. A privileged attendant at births and deaths, often first on the scene at tragedy, you cared for people when they were most vulnerable—when they were sick, injured, or dying. And believe it or not, even today, over a hundred years after you began your practice here, people still remember you and are most grateful."

Stepping away from the Zeien plot, I knew what I had come for. The old *North Branch Reviews* were true. I could now believe in the microfilm world, that odd celluloid record of North Branch that gave me such a vivid picture of this small town on the sand plain. It seemed marvelous to me that time had not disbanded the community, that its members had not scattered to the four winds. I wondered if the same would be true of the present community. It seemed unlikely. Communities today are more fluid—like patterns created by the colored glass shards of a kaleidoscope, they form and collapse, reform and collapse again, constantly in flux. Few people stay in one place.

As I reached the gravel road bisecting the cemetery, I turned to survey the scene. The community that had once been woven together by friendship, commerce, marriage, and common endeavor remained a community in death. It lay not, however, in a cluster of headstones being eroded by the sand. The community was now in the soil, part of the soil, fading away unseen. It was becoming earth and oak trees.

Two

Oak Savanna

THE EARLY RESIDENTS OF NORTH BRANCH carved their community out of oak savanna, a biological transition zone between the lush eastern deciduous forest and the equally lush but treeless tallgrass prairie of the continent's midsection. They carved it as a sculptor chisels a granite block, chipping away first this portion, then that. They carved and whittled until, like a sculpted piece, it bore little resemblance to the parent material. One must look hard to find the trace remains of savanna.

The midwestern oak savanna—what some call "oak openings"— once extended through the middle of the North American continent, from Minnesota to Texas. In Minnesota, it cut a diagonal from the state's northwestern corner through its center to the confluence of the Mississippi and Minnesota Rivers. Reminiscent of a park—indeed, savannas are often referred to as "parklands"— it enchanted early European explorers, who rhapsodized over the landscape.

"The country through which we passed is delightful in the extreme," wrote Dr. Douglas Houghton in 1832 as he floated down the Mississippi through central Minnesota with the Schoolcraft expedition.

"The country around is prairie, with post oak," observed the Reverend Boutwell of that same party. "The whole country is the most inviting to emigrants and [the most] interesting of any part of the United States that I have seen."

But there was more to the savanna than a pleasing countenance. The landscape presented an eerie wistfulness, a sense of déjà vu, which Mr. Boutwell discerned: "[it exhibits] an appearance of a country that has been cultivated for centuries and is now deserted by its inhabitants."

It was one of the duties of the Schoolcraft expedition to scout out possible agricultural land, and everyone noted that the savanna would make good farmland—easy to clear, the light soil yielding to the plow. Their remarks proved prescient: by the turn of the next century, little savanna remained in North America. Oak savanna is now the rarest of Minnesota's major ecosystems. Preserved parcels are few and far between, but one of the best is only twenty miles from North Branch, in northern Anoka County.

The Helen Allison Savanna is an eighty-acre parcel of land that was a far-sighted purchase by the Nature Conservancy in 1960. Even forty years ago, it was considered a rare example of bur oak savanna on sand because it contained the original prairie understory. The proximity of the University of Minnesota's Cedar Creek research station figured prominently in its preservation. The land, which is directly across a rural road from Cedar Creek, had been "discovered" by a researcher in 1959. Dr. Roger Bray, a specialist in oak savanna vegetation, realized that the small parcel's lack of disturbance made it a priceless jewel. Together with other university botanists, he approached the Nature Conservancy for acquisition. When the Minnesota chapter of the Nature Conservancy bought the land for $3,500, it became one of the first prairie tracts in its holdings. Three years later, the Nature Conservancy conducted a prescribed burn to restore native vegetation, the first time the organization had ever used this now common restorative practice.

As is true of many Nature Conservancy tracts, the preserve has been turned over to the Minnesota Department of Natural Resources to manage as a Scientific and Natural Area. Such areas are regarded as the "crown jewels" in Minnesota's array of state-managed lands.

The preserve is named for a researcher at the University of Minnesota herbarium, Helen Lowry Allison. Pursuing a lifelong passion for grasses, Ms. Allison had worked with university professors on grass identification as a second career. She was one of several who donated money to purchase the tract, one of several whose fervor for the prairie world led them to devote their lives to knowing and preserving it.

We first sought out this gem of a savanna on a golden late October day, when all green had drained from the landscape, replaced by the warm tones of fall. We had lived in North Branch for six years. By then, I was already in love with the large, twisted bur oaks that graced our neighborhood and I had already come to understand how they had been cherished by past North Branchers. Places in town were named for the oaks—there was the Oak Inn, on Main Street, and Oak Hill Cemetery, just north of it. We ourselves lived on Oak Street, under the shade of five shaggy trees that periodically dropped their prickly-capped acorns for us to rake.

Notably, there were no places named after savanna grasses—no Bluestem Boulevard, no Big Blue Bowling Alley—but we had discovered remnant grasses, too, less than a block from our house. We appreciated these wild grasses, the ancient partners of our bur oaks, and were pleased they were still around.

The Helen Allison Savanna was fenced in, though we weren't sure why. Like the Great Wall of China, the fence could serve either to contain its wildness or to ward off invaders. We weren't sure a mere barricade could do either. At the entrance someone had erected a mailbox on a wooden post, and inside we found a visitors' log on which was scrawled, in pencil, a list of names. Many were re-peat visitors who came often to this place. Sometimes they added commentary on the phenological events they had witnessed: "April 24—pasque flowers in bloom," one entry read. Apparently, Helen Allison had many devoted admirers. We added our names to the list.

As we made our way into the preserve, we identified a silhou-ette of red and pin oaks off in the distance. Surrounding us on ei-ther side of the path and waving gracefully over our heads were towering, slender stalks of Indian grass. On far-off sand dunes to the west, we spied big bluestem—another tallgrass—growing in sparse clusters, patches of fine, light sand showing between plants. In some places, little bluestem, another familiar grass, grew in thick bunches. The little blues had taken on a fall coloration of rich, deep wine. The seed heads, thick with fine, hairlike awns, captured the light, creating a halo around each head. It gave the bunches of grass a fuzzy appearance, soft and strokeable, like fur.

The chimerical quality of a savanna—half-prairie, half-forest—makes it an area capable of harboring a high diversity of plants and animals. Prairie species thrive in open areas, but forest plants are at home in the sun-dappled shade beneath the oaks. Helen Alli-son's plant list numbers over two hundred species, some of them rare, on a mere eighty acres.

On our hands and knees we uncovered the more subtle members of the savanna community. We identified the brown, curling remains of butterfly milkweed and hoary puccoon. Leadplant, woody and ro-bust, was still a silvery gray. American hazel, forming a shrub layer under groupings of oaks, sported tiny, dry catkins that attracted chick-adees. As we crouched down low, we scrutinized the sand that served as soil. It was a pale, creamy color, with little humic content. We won-dered what kind of nutrition it offered the plants. Later, we learned that, indeed, Helen Allison starved its oaks. The trees on the preserve are strikingly stunted and misshapen. Some, estimated to be a century old, stand only six feet high. They appear crabbed and wizened, as if they've endured a great deal.

Nevertheless, they were in their glory that October day. Oaks persist in their greenery, clinging tenaciously to their chlorophyll long after maples and ashes have turned color and dropped leaves. Here, in late fall, the red oaks were crimson- and claret-colored. Bur and pin oaks, not as flashy as their cousins, had turned butterscotch- and caramel-colored, the rich, warm hues of autumn layered upon each other.

We spent the afternoon happily wandering about the small tract. The rolling terrain, with its dunes and swales, made the savanna seem bigger than it actually was. We had a sense of isolation, stillness, and solitude that day, incongruent with the savanna's size and the degree of development surrounding it.

The savanna did not disappoint us. What we saw all around was a diversity of plants unimaginably greater than anywhere else we had been in our six years of living on the sand plain. We were dazzled by the intricacy set before our eyes: the dry remains of many grass species, some that we knew by sight, others that looked familiar, encountered in a long-ago botany lab, and some that were new to us; the delicately preserved forbs—prairie flowers—that retained characteristic shapes in desiccated form; the mini-habitats of swale, dune, upland, and marsh. We had only begun to explore the wonders of this savanna. We now knew why Helen Allison had so many admirers.

Back at home, I became haunted by memories of our visit. Images of the trees, the shaggy grass, the rolling hills played on my mind like ghosts. Perhaps it was the appearance of previous human occupation, akin to the strange perception described by Reverend Boutwell. Probably it was in part due to the recognition that our neighborhood in North Branch had once looked like that—that I could now envision the town's beginning, the coming of the railroad, the first settlers, the first houses, having seen the land as it had been.

Later, I became aware that I retained a deeper, older sense of being at home on the savanna, that this sense was lodged in my childhood. I recalled gravitating to a thin line of pin oaks that resolutely clung to a railroad cut south of my elementary school. My childhood home in the Twin Cities—Minneapolis and St. Paul—had once been savanna. It had taken me thirty years to realize this.

The savanna in spring wears her dreariest garb. Prairie grasses are known as "hot weather" grasses, slow to green up and send forth new shoots. In early May, the savanna lacks the freshness of spring woodlands. The grasses are straw-colored and lusterless, matted from the winter's snows, without a hint of new life. Pasqueflowers, the first flowers of spring, bloom in April but fade within a week. By mid-May, they are faint and papery, assuming the color and texture of the grasses in which they nestle. Nevertheless, we made a pilgrimage to the Helen Allison Savanna one Mother's Day. The afternoon was mild and bright, and our sun-hungry souls longed to be outdoors, without the encumbrance of jackets and sweaters, in the easy warmth of May.

On this Mother's Day expedition, we took along our four children, ages two to nine. As we piled in the mini-van, the mood was festive and expectant: we would take a hike on the savanna to celebrate spring!

Helen Allison looked exhausted, as if the winter had been too much for her. In stark contrast to the bright green grass and blooming apple trees that were already enlivening our yard in North Branch, the savanna was subdued and brown. The oaks, tentative in catkins but leafless, could not shade us from the bright, hot sun. It was not a sylvan delight, and the children, lacking our discerning, trained eyes, were reluctant to embark on a long, boring hike over acres and acres of dead grass.

Nevertheless, we insisted (it was *Mother's Day*, after all) and coaxed them into the interior, heading for the pasqueflowers, for lack of a better destination. It had been a snowy winter and a wet spring. The swales held melt and rainwater, which formed temporary vernal ponds in the depressions of the rolling landscape. The ponds were clear and reflected the sky, bright patches of blue amid the straw-colored grass. The children were drawn to the water, far more attractive than dry, old grass. By the time we adults had arrived at the water's edge with the younger children, the older ones had already taken off their shoes and socks, ready to wade. But their attraction to the water was mild compared to their delight upon discovery that it held scores of tiny, little frogs, and that these frogs fit wonderfully well into their tiny, little hands.

Soon, both frogs and children were hopping at the edge of the pond. Now it was my turn to be delighted. The kids were catching a variety of species. Delicate, pale-colored spring peepers, hardly an inch long, were the most abundant. Classified as tree frogs, peepers sing out in high, bird-like peeps day and night during their breeding season. From their dainty toes clad in rounded toe pads to their diminutive snouts, they are among the smallest of the frogs, enchanting miniatures

Our eldest brought me a gray tree frog, slightly larger and identifiable by the bright orange patch on its inner hind legs. There are two species of gray tree frogs in our area, so similar that they are distinguished in the field only by their calls. This one, securely enclosed within a boy's cupped hands, looked rather grumpy, not in the mood for singing. It remained anonymous.

Then our five-year-old captured a knobby-backed toad up on a hill away from the pond and came running, very pleased with himself. Together we peered at the little creature crouched in the well made by John's fingers and thumbs. It peered back at us with beady black eyes. There is something endearing about toads. They are humble animals, plain and dumpy, odd amphibian incarnations of Winston Churchill. This one appeared to be smiling because of its rounded, toothless lips.

A brilliant green leopard frog remained prudently out of reach of the exuberant frog catchers. I went after that one so the children could examine it closely and observe the range of differences in the savanna's frogs, but the leopard frog, eyes half-shut, positioned itself just beyond arm's reach. It hung suspended in the water, escaping with a perfect frog kick every time I got close.

We tallied six species of frogs and toads that afternoon, including the northern chorus frogs we could hear singing in the distance and the elegant, masked wood frog we later saw hopping under a cluster of oaks. In a decade during which frog populations around the world were crashing, the wealth of amphibious life on the savanna astonished and delighted us. We were once again dazzled by the unexpected intricacy of the untouched natural world.

By early June, the oaks of Helen Allison are in full leaf. The thick mat of grass roots, long dormant under the chaff of last year's growth, have once more put out slender new shoots, nascent grasses that will soon become a waving sea of green. There is a fresh-faced countenance to the savanna in early summer, enhanced by early morning sunlight. We drank in the loveliness one Saturday morning as a group of volunteers gathered near the sign-in stand to participate in a work day held by the Nature Conservancy.

As a reward for being willing to give up a precious Saturday to pull weeds, we were first treated to a tour of the preserve, led by field botanist Barb Delaney. Highly skilled in taxonomy, the identification of species, Barb was at that time involved in the state biological survey of Anoka County's plants and was thus conversant with the many species known to grow at Helen Allison. Dark-haired and slender, Barb had the eyes of a scholar behind wire-rimmed glasses, and she spoke deliberately and carefully, a well-trained scientist. We had known each other from our graduate school days at the University of Minnesota, and she had impressed me then with her vast knowledge about Minnesota plant life.

Also in attendance was an elderly, round-shouldered man sporting a black beret. I recognized him as Dr. Donald Lawrence, a retired professor of ecology at the University of Minnesota. Dr. Lawrence was prominent for his pioneering work on ecological succession at Glacier Bay, Alaska. Among a certain set, he was considered a living legend. I was mildly surprised to see him here. He had seemed old to me in the 1970s, when I had been at the U. He must now be well over eighty, I calculated. He had prepared handouts that included a timeline of historical activity affecting the Helen Allison Savanna and a short description of its acquisition by the Nature Conservancy. As I skimmed the pages, I saw that Dr. Lawrence had been instrumental in preserving the tract. He had paid out the earnest money to secure the purchase in 1960 and he had also, I suspected, drawn up the detailed timeline, which noted specific times at which a non-native species of plant had been introduced. I pondered an image of the great Dr. Lawrence carefully watching over this small patch of earth for over thirty years, and it moved me. It would seem that famous scientists are meant for greater work. Perhaps preserving a pristine eighty acres was greatness enough.

Barb walked us over the savanna's topographical features, up the hills that had once been sand dunes, down into the swales between them that had held water and singing frogs only a month before. We paused on top of one hill. Below we could see blow-out areas, large patches of sand devoid of vegetation. We learned that the dry years of the 1930s had reactivated dune-building at Helen Allison. Drought following drought had discouraged the growth of plants on the sand, plants whose roots had, in the past, elongated and probed deep into the soil, seeking water. These roots had anchored the sand, preventing it from shifting and allowing other plants to establish themselves until the now stationary dune supported a diverse grass community. But the dry spell of the 1930s had changed that stability. Blow-out areas, located on the windward face of the dunes, dotted the interior of the savanna now; sixty intervening years of normal rainfall hadn't been sufficient to bring back an anchoring grass cover.

Nevertheless, some plants clung. One of these was false heather (*Hudsonia tomentosa*), tough and spidery, sprawling haphazardly over the sand. Its precarious appearance was misleading—a deep, woody root tethered it to firm substrate lying below the sand layer. Barb's slender fingers gently gave the homely plant a tug as she drew our attention to it. Despite its lack of beauty or showiness, *Hudsonia* is held in special regard by savanna aficionados. It is one of only two plants in Minnesota whose distribution runs on the southeast/northwest diagonal, following the path of the state's savanna.

The other, hoary frostweed (*Helianthemum Bicknellii*), was just coming up, though not on a blow-out. We located its white and green leaves on a fully vegetated portion of the oak savanna where the growing conditions had not been so severe. Both of these species had been given special recognition when Minnesota botanists Gerald Ownbey and Thomas Morley chose to include maps of the species' unique distribution on the title page of of their classic book, *Vascular Plants of Minnesota*.

Barb was passionate about plants, and her focused, serious demeanor became animated with each new find. "Ah!" she exclaimed at one point, fondling a short, stiff plant with affection. "Here's Muhlenberg's sedge!" It was clear she was among those captivated by Helen Allison's charms.

As the morning sun rose higher, those of us who had been viewing the scenery of the savanna as tourists transformed ourselves into patrons, protectors of its integrity. Now on the lookout for non-native invaders, we laid hand lenses and clipboards aside and donned work gloves.

I was familiar with the two chief offenders: goat's beard and sweet clover, both already in flower. Goat's beard produces showy, lemony flowers that metamorphose into giant "dandelion" heads of fluffy, cottony seeds. Sweet clover, a lacy, aggressive weed with fragrant white or yellow blossoms, known to city and country dweller alike, grows abundantly along roadsides and in vacant lots. Although goat's beard is unquestionably attractive, and although I frequently cut sweet clover for bouquets, our actions this morning were not based on aesthetics. We understood that these European natives had the capacity to infiltrate the pristine oak savanna at Helen Allison and wreak havoc.

We couldn't use herbicides. There are none specific to these two persistent, successful species, and a general herbicide would threaten the precious natives—as well as their pollinating insects.

So we pulled by hand, uprooting the plants and leaving their roots high and dry, exposed to the sun, resulting, we hoped, in death.

The most likely threat of invasion into Helen Allison occurs along the northern and eastern boundaries of the preserve, defined by county roads. These dry, disturbed roadsides are well suited to weedy species—and the European species that have become established on this continent are almost always weedy: resistant to drought, short-lived, capable of producing copious amounts of seeds. It was important to get to the goat's beard and sweet clover before the flowers matured and produced seeds.

Dr. Lawrence's timeline of the historic events at Helen Allison informed us that this hand pulling of weeds had been going on for twenty years. In 1974, volunteers had commenced combat on non-native invaders, going after sweet clover and hoary alyssum and also mullein, a tall, fuzzy-leafed invader of abandoned fields Mullein is so ubiquitous in Minnesota, its tall, buttery-yellow flower head so familiar, that many are surprised to learn it is nonnative. But Dr. Lawrence had scrawled his opinion of mullein (an uncomplimentary version of cartoon swearing *#!!) in the margins of the handout and underlined that its seeds can remain viable in the soil for at least fifty years.

Any gardener can tell you that the battle with weeds is never over. Unwelcome plants are considered weeds precisely because of their tendency to grow quickly, reproduce prolifically, and invade open areas (like gardens). But it is discouraging, as well as eye opening, to pull weeds for the Nature Conservancy and realize that simply preserving the land is not enough to keep a beleaguered savanna intact. It will take constant vigilance to maintain Helen Allison's natural abundance of grasses and flowers, of insects and frogs.

It may seem strange to consider Helen Allison an island, but that is precisely what it is: eighty acres of native oak savanna in a sea of manmade environment—lawns and driveways, roads and parking lots. Island biogeography theory tells us that islands suffer a high rate of extinction simply by random processes. Small populations on an island, separated from the rest of their kind, can be done in by genetic mishaps or eliminated by chance and are particularly susceptible to invasion by aggressive species which out-compete them for resources. Seen in this light, and applying predictive theory, the long-term future does not look good for Helen Allison.

Still, the savanna endures in our time. It is a living legacy, the best we can afford, to hand our children and other Americans who will follow us. It is a testimony to the vibrant intricacy of Mother Earth and an inspiration to all who attempt to preserve and restore our remaining wild land.

Bur Oak

ON AN OPEN STRETCH OF LIMESTONE CLIFF along busy State Highway 55, a cluster of slender bur oaks clings to life. Ravaged by time and the prevailing northwest wind, they look out of place, and they are. The trees are a ragged last piece of the oak savanna that occupied the bluff land overlooking the confluence of the Minnesota and Mississippi Rivers before the coming of the Europeans.

The parent trees, dropping the acorns that became these oaks, might have been present when Zebulon Pike led an expedition to this spot in 1805 and secured land from the Dakota for a future fort. They may have been saplings when Fort Snelling was constructed in 1819, may have witnessed the growth of a small community, St. Anthony, from a sawmill site on the Mississippi into the city of Minneapolis. Certainly, these existing bur oaks were alive when Minneapolis pressed outward, engulfing and transforming the savanna until it had been whittled down to the thinnest fringe. Now these bereft trees, standing alone, define what is meant by the term *savanna*.

The bur oaks survived the construction of Wold-Chamberlain Field in 1923 and remained upright as the two-lane road into the airport grew to four lanes, then six. They even survived its transformation into the roaring thoroughfare that today carries all travelers to and from Minnesota's main airport.

My eyes seek out the bur oaks on each trip to the airport. By the time I arrive at its entrance, I have already become uneasy by the increase in complexity and confusion typified by the route I take to get there—from the quiet county road running past our house to the state highway threading through Chisago County to the thundering interstate muscling southward into the metropolitan area. I rely on the bur oaks, their scraggly, tenacious forms, to remind me of who I am, of where I come from and of what will be waiting for me when I return. They tell me that being rooted in one place is a good thing, that it enables a body to endure endless change.

The bur oak marks Minnesota's savanna like the saguaro cactus identifies the Sonoran Desert. It is the North American savanna's signature tree. Rough barked and craggy, with branches that twist and knot, it is an appropriate species to serve as the outpost of the eastern deciduous forest. Although bur oaks grow on a variety of soil types and are actually considered by some to be most at home in moist river bottoms, they, along with red oaks, are the oaks of the oak savanna. The most northern of all North American oaks and the most drought resistant, bur oaks range from Texas north into Canada.

Life on the sand plain's oak savanna presents difficulties. The coarse-grained soil holds little water and is droughty, and sand shifts with the wind, providing an unstable substrate. In the past, spring fires swept through the savanna, favoring prairie grasses but eliminating most trees. To flourish on the Anoka Sand Plain, trees must rise to the challenge.

Several of the bur oak's distinctive features enable this tree to do well on the sand plain. The first is a relatively thick cork layer underneath its bark. Most trees have cork, but oaks have especially thick layers (indeed, those indispensable little plugs in wine bottles come from oak cork), which give them protection from light fires, so that oaks can grow on prairies, where maples cannot. The other notable attribute is its taproot. A bur acorn falling in late summer or autumn immediately sends out a small root shoot that fingers down through the soil. This shoot, which will become the tree's dominant taproot, both anchors the nascent oak and provides it with an underlying source of water. Winter follows and the acorn becomes dormant. After the season's cold—the acorn requires chilling to sprout—an aerial shoot appears, transforming the seed into a seedling. The seedling might remain leafless and undetected for several years. When it finally sports two full sized leaves, the taproot will be many feet deep.

The remarkable taproot, so essential to the survival of a bur oak, is the main reason the tree has proven tricky to transplant. By the time a bur oak is a respectable size for landscaping, the taproot can't be squeezed into any pot. Consequently, bur oaks are mainly wild trees, seeded by nature (often by squirrels) and not placed on most sites by human hand. When I see a large bur oak in Minnesota—in a south Minneapolis yard, for example, or in a St. Cloud city park—I feel a small, visceral thrill and think, "Aha! This was oak savanna!"

It is not difficult to develop a penchant for bur oaks: their dark, contorted branches opening to a broad crown have a rough but satisfying beauty. Our North Branch house is shaded by five mature bur oaks, some of the many trees in the neighborhood that give "Oak Street" its name.

I had never before lived in the company of oaks, had never gazed day after day on their lovely forms, so my appreciation of them is an acquired taste. I grew up on cleared pastureland. My father had transplanted sugar maples and basswoods from the wood lot of our ancestral Wisconsin farm to shade our Minnesota yard. I was accustomed to the refinement of these Big Woods trees—the saplings and we kids grew up together. I remember them as unsubstantial, anchored by stakes against the wind, ineffective at casting shade.

However, the other significant trees of my childhood had genuine bearing: mature white pines surrounding the family cabin in central Minnesota. Stately and graceful, they captured my imagination at an early age. I formed a flaming passion for them. They were friends; they provided solace. They seemed eternal, in contrast to the maple saplings, which were clearly newcomers.

And then, in my thirties, I met the oaks. In the dog days of summer, the oaks cast a cooling shade over the house and lawn. In the winter, when their craggy silhouettes stand stark against twilight's pastels, their comely form takes my breath away.

In shade and silhouette, however, the oaks are not totally dissimilar from other trees. What really sets them apart is their prodigious production of acorns. Bur oaks take their name from the peculiarities of their seed. Their acorn caps bristle with burlike fringe, reminding me of tiny wooly hats pulled low over little faces. Their scientific name, *Quercus macrocarpa*, also refers to the acorn: *Quercus* is the generic name for all oaks; *macrocarpa* means "large seed."

In his book *Trees: Their Natural History*, Peter Thomas spends some time musing over the advantages of having a large seed. A seed, the link between generations, must be able to do two things: it needs to be large enough to give the seedling a good start, and it needs to be able to move some distance from the parent, to disperse into the wider world. Some trees, like birch, have tiny seeds that scatter in the wind, but trees whose seedlings will take root under dense shade, like oak and beech, tend to have large seeds. These seedlings need bigger stored supplies of energy and nutrients to become established and the reserves necessary to grow a root rapidly, giving them a better chance to reach water. The big seed lends the neophyte a little competitive edge in the battle for savanna turf.

On the other hand, there are disadvantages to large acorns.

Some animals zero in on the nutritious morsels for a large portion of their diet. Woodland species, like tree squirrels and white-tailed deer, and prairie species, such as the thirteen-lined ground squirrel (a.k.a. the Minnesota "gopher"), dine on bur acorns. A squirrel's inclination to cache and then fail to retrieve acorn stores, however, helps disseminate the seeds.

Bur oaks usually produce a staggering amount of acorns one year and almost none for the year or two following. This phenomenon, called "masting," occurs synchronously with other oaks in the area. When our oaks have a "good year," everyone else is inundated with acorns, too. The *scritch, scritch* of broom rakes trying futilely to remove the heavy acorns from sidewalks and struggling lawns can be heard throughout the neighborhood.

Outside my window, the bur oaks ready themselves for spring Long after our crab apple has exploded into showy bloom and the soft maple has fresh, youthful leaves, the stodgy bur oaks eke out cautious brushes of yellow-green catkins. Full leaves will follow in a week or so. Catkins are an oak tree's flowers, the first step in the production of acorns. The staminate (male) flowers are most prominent. Long and feathery, they are fuzzy with yellow pollen, a high-energy food source. In mid-May, when migrating birds are in the middle of their spring journey, I awaken each morning to the song of a new species enjoying a repast in the treetops. Orioles, vireos, warblers—everyone dines at the bur oak café.

I thrill most to the coming of the Tennessee warblers. I always hear Tennessees before I see them. "Chip chip chickachick-achicka," I think I hear them chatter. For a small bird, a Tennessee warbler can produce an amazing volume of continuous noise—it would be charitable to call it "song." Tennessees are small, edgy birds that flit nervously from branch to branch, foraging for insects and devouring catkins. With gray-toned breasts and greenish backs, they are elusive in the treetops. Attracted to the highest branches, they are notorious for giving bird watchers "warbler neck." Through binoculars, I watch them from our second-story windows. They busily work the catkins with their thin, black bills. They have a right to their ravenous appetites: Tennessees migrate from Central America, a two-thousand-mile journey made mostly at night, navigating by starlight. North Branch is only a pit stop for them. They are headed for Canada's north woods.

In a week or so, the birds will be gone and the oak leaves will be noticeable. They first appear in beguiling miniature with tiny veins and indentations. As quickly as Minnesota's spring becomes summer, the leaves grow to full size and the tree is dressed for June.

Our five oaks and those of our neighbor, Mildred Bloom, form a shady grove. They are all about the same size and must be about the same age, perhaps springing up together in a year when the weather favored acorn germination. I whimsically imagine the workings of one busy squirrel, burying acorns willy-nilly in scattered mounds produced by a burrowing pocket gopher, the two rodents unwitting gardeners producing our grove.

One spring, despite their imperturbable size, the oaks were in jeopardy. The city of North Branch had decided to widen Oak Street to accommodate increased traffic to the medical clinic. The new road—a thoroughfare, really—threatened the largest Bloom tree, an immense oak over two feet in diameter. Little pink flags clustered ominously at its base.

Alarmed, the neighbors flooded city hall with pleas to save the aged oak and other neighborhood trees in the proposed road's path. The city planner had wanted a commercial district street, but we argued the case for a shady, narrow, neighborhood road. The mayor (who was, of course, related to some of the neighbors) was surprisingly receptive, and somehow the matter was settled within the day. The old oak was granted a stay of execution.

However, that was not the end of the old oak's woes. The project had been not merely to widen the road but also to put in a storm sewer and replace existing water lines. Surveyors were baffled by their calculations in the Bloom yard: the water line seemed to run *through* the oak's root system. How could this be? The Bloom house had been connected to city water for fewer than sixty years, and the oak was definitely older than that. They concluded that the city had deliberately run the water line through the tree when the houses had been hooked up to the water system. From my window, I watched the general contractor and his assistant circle the tree, gazing at its crown, and I feared the worst. It would be easiest to cut it down. I thought of the female wood duck that had nestled in its boughs just that morning, protected by the old tree for perhaps the last time.

A third and final worry plagued the tree: the specter of oak wilt. Oak wilt is a fungal disease affecting primarily red oaks, but bur oaks can also be susceptible. The disease is spread only in a two-month period, between mid-April and mid-June, during which time oak trees should not be trimmed or injured, actions opening them up to the fungus. The road project would do more than that the tree's exposed roots would be cut as new pipe was laid, an assault on the oak's defenses at a vulnerable time.

No one had calculated in the oak wilt susceptibility period when the project plans were drawn up. Back we neighbors went to the city council, not really expecting them to delay the project but wanting to make them aware of poor planning. A delay was unthinkable to them. One councilman growled, "We're not going to delay the project for a *tree!*" And they didn't.

But we had made a point. The project's general contractor treated the oaks with solicitous care. When it came time to work on the aged Bloom oak, he did not cut it down but instead had the workmen slip the new copper pipe inside the existing water line and set the valve far up on the lawn, away from the root system. He invited me to peer into the hole with him, where the roots of the massive tree lay uncovered. We could see the lead pipe running through the tangled mass, a bizarre intertwining of the natural and the human-made. Roots and pipe had peacefully co-existed for sixty years and would continue to do so for perhaps sixty more. The staid old tree had held a secret and would continue to hold it, waiting to be discovered by the next generation of North Branchers when they replaced the water lines.

It has been nearly a decade since the Oak Street project, and all the oaks are alive and flourishing. None of them contracted wilt, nor even lost branches. We watered the trees religiously that first summer, trying to help them recover from the cut roots. It was a little like nursing elephants, monstrous organisms that dwarfed our puny selves. The Bloom oak is also among the living, producing vast amounts of acorns every other year. Day in and day out, it harbors the usual assortment of nuthatches, chickadees, and blue jays. This spring I noticed a band of robins and fox sparrows foraging on the lawn around its trunk. They were feasting on bits of acorns left over from the fall.

Bull Snake!

THE BOLDLY PATTERNED SNAKE, its back bright
with blotches of black, brown, and ochre, stretched nearly the
width of the road—or so it appeared. Intent on crossing, madly wiggling back and forth as it headed to the other side, it moved
earnestly, purposefully, as if worried it might not make it to safety.

I was in my car on the gravel road leading from the town of
Sunrise to the landing on the St. Croix River. It was a dry, golden
day in late September, and we were preparing for a paddle on the
river. The lovely Sunrise Cemetery, one of the oldest in Chisago
County, shaded by towering white pines, seemed to be the snake's
destination.

Part of me stared in amazement as I apprehended its size—at
least six feet long, the longest snake I had ever seen outside a zoo,
longer than any snake I'd seen in the Everglades. Its girth was
tremendous—as thick as my upper arm. Another part of me wondered what ungodly noise was filling the interior of my car. Surely

it couldn't be *my* voice emitting the shrieks, the rich, throaty cries of terror. My mother had taught me not to scream. "Susan!" she had scolded whenever I'd cry out during play. "Stop that! You sound like a fishwife!" I had been so thoroughly conditioned, in fact, that I had occasionally wondered if I would be able to scream if ever I needed to. I shouldn't have worried.

My little Honda halted in front of the writhing body. From the safe distance of my car, I could see that it was a bull snake, *Pituophis catenifer*, a snake fairly common to Minnesota prairies and oak savannas. Bull snakes tend to bask along roadsides on sunny afternoons, as if taking pleasure in the last days of autumn before descending into winter hibernation. That's probably what this one was doing before my car roared up and disturbed its nap.

It isn't hard to identify a bull snake. No other Minnesota snake grows to such dimensions. It's not surprising, then, that the bull snake also has the distinction of being the first Minnesota reptile with a published sighting. Father Hennepin recorded encountering "a huge Serpent as big as a Man's leg, and seven or eight feet long" near the mouth of the Minnesota River during his travels to the region in 1679–80. This creature later caused him to have terrible dreams.

Like many people, I have a "thing" about snakes. I'm disinclined to call it a phobia, though I suppose that's what it is. It doesn't stem from any early traumatic encounters with serpents, though there were snakes in my childhood. We had a resident garter snake that hung out in our rhubarb patch and sometimes in the cluster of wild roses adjacent to our garden. Once this shy, docile animal slithered over my friend Diane's big toe as we walked barefoot on the sidewalk—we both retain that forty-year-old memory! Snakes in the window wells, snakes on the rock pile, snakes in the hands of small boys on the playground—these events did not inflict psychological wounds.

No, I suspect the source of my phobia flows from a much deeper well. I have a hunch that it traces back to the childhood of our race, the dawn of *Homo sapiens*, or even earlier. In her classic work with chimpanzees, Jane Goodall found that chimps responded aggressively toward pythons out of aversion, following initial fear. She observed them chasing slow-moving snakes for some distance, wielding sticks as clubs. Old World monkeys, and apes in general, noisily communicate the presence of snakes to others in their group. Primates in general, it seems, have a "thing" about snakes.

Zoologist E. O. Wilson points out that the most common phobias concern elements that were potentially dangerous in our evolutionary past—snakes, spiders, rats, cliffs. In his book *Biophilia*, he discusses a study of identical twins that indicated genetic factors played a major role in establishing animal phobias. (He also relates a charming story of his own twins, who as toddlers developed a strong affinity for a snake they found.) A genetic tendency to acquire such a phobia would add extra insurance that the individual will stay out of harm's way. I like to think that rather than possessing an irrational fear, I am instead intensely in tune with my natural self.

My aversion to snakes was once so strong that I nearly didn't major in biology. However, over years of repeated exposure, my phobia has eased. No doubt handling dozens of pickled snakes, stored in jars of formaldehyde, helped lessen it, as did years of biological fieldwork. Now, after the initial unpleasant surprise of discovering a snake as it wiggles away, I often pursue it to identify it, to admire its coloration, or simply to take in its face, noting the family resemblance to turtles, which I love. But I am still not interested in a close, personal relationship with snakes.

I did not have these thoughts, however, when I confronted my six-foot snaky friend. At that moment, I did not consider how splendidly it represented the reptiles of the oak savanna. Nor did I think of its affinity to sandy soils—how it spends much of its time resting in rodent burrows, how it can burrow through the sand, using its snout as a shovel. I was not interested in how it traps its small rodent prey against tunnel walls until they suffocate, or how it handles larger prey in its constricting coils.

I wasn't inclined to remember how individualistic bull snakes can be in confrontation—most slipping away toward the nearest burrow, some becoming ornery when cornered, vibrating their tails like rattlesnakes, hissing loudly (the *best* hissers, one reference book claimed) and striking repeatedly, capable of administering a painful bite. I didn't think about how they will den with timber rattlers in winter, in those parts of Minnesota where the two species occur together.

And I didn't remember, either, that their numbers are declining in Minnesota, partly from habitat loss, to the point that the state's Department of Natural Resources lists them as a species of "special concern." No, watching from my car, I had but one thought: I could destroy this scary snake, by one of the means most responsible for their decline—death from an automobile.

Of course, I didn't. Instead, I watched it slither away into the cemetery. I've never killed a snake on purpose, and on accident I've run over only two or three. It bothers me intensely when I do. All living creatures want so desperately to live; my empathy for their plight runs deeper than my fear. I have trouble killing any animal larger than a mosquito.

If that bull snake wants to live in the Sunrise cemetery, that's fine with me. *I'm* not going back there.

Pocket Gophers

MY INTRODUCTION TO POCKET GOPHERS came early in life and was bloody and violent, a stark contrast to my otherwise gentle childhood. Our yard in the burgeoning suburb of Roseville was carved out of abandoned pastureland. To its north lay ten acres of remaining pasture, overgrown with non-native grass, goldenrod, and wild rose. This untended field harbored small wild animals. On cold February days, we could hear the raucous calls of bold cock pheasants as they corralled their harems of meek, docile hens. On spring mornings, we listened for the sweet, flute-like song of western meadowlarks, which nested in the field. Running unrestrained through the waist-high grass, we came upon the soft, friable earth of pocket gopher mounds, signs of the burrowing rodents that made their living munching the roots and stems of old-field plants.

This essay might have rhapsodized on peace and harmony with nature had the pocket gophers kept to themselves, but that is not their way. There was the matter of my father's garden, enticingly laid out at the edge of the field. In it grew potatoes and carrots, beets, onions, and strawberries—all manner of luscious fruits and vegetables, undoubtedly as tempting to the pocket gophers as Eve's apple was to Adam. Every year, one or two would burrow into Dad's garden, announcing their presence with two fan-shaped mounds of fine-particled soil that appeared overnight. Once—this is no joke— Dad watched his row of beets disappear one by one, as in a Road Runner cartoon, a pocket gopher moving, unseen in its tunnel, down the line, pulling the delicate morsels out of sight into the soil.

A country boy by upbringing, Dad had his means of dealing with pocket gophers. The most direct method employed a pan trap with nasty iron jaws that clenched the unsuspecting gopher's leg in a way not approved of by the People for Ethical Treatment of Animals. Dad stored these heavy iron traps on pegs in the garage. At first sight of a mound, he'd haul the traps out to the garden, spread apart their jagged jaws, and set them inside the gopher's tunnels, covering the hole with a board so the gopher wouldn't suspect any disturbance. I'd tag along and watch him dig into the tunnel from the mound, lay out the trap, and set it, but I didn't hang around for Part Two. Part Two was when he caught the gopher a day or two later, alive and wiggling at the end of the trap. He'd whack the animal over the head with my brother's baseball bat, then bury it in a far corner of the garden, an earthy end for an earthy animal.

The pan trap was pioneer technology for a pioneer problem: people cultivating soil where gophers once had free rein. Later, anti-gopher technology became more sophisticated. In my teens, Dad acquired a different kind of trap with a name worthy of Agatha Christie: the Death Klutch Trap. The Death Klutch Trap had the advantage (to the trapper) of killing the gopher by skewering it through the neck with a set of wicked spikes. Whether it was more humane than a pan trap, a gopher would have to say.

Dad also used an indirect method of gopher elimination: the poison peanut. Not peanuts at all, but round, appetizing pellets laced with strychnine, they came in a black-and-white canister, the label printed with a dramatic miniature skull and crossbones, which impressed me to no end. Dad would shake out five or six "peanuts," and, with a metal scoop used expressly for this one purpose, slide them into the tunnel. But poison peanuts were an unsatisfying way of dealing with pocket gophers because (unlike in murder mysteries) there was no corpse providing proof of elimination. The gopher simply disappeared—that is to say, the mounds stopped appearing—but it was entirely possible that the gopher had merely moved on and would be back, later, perhaps when the beets were larger and Dad was away on vacation at the cabin. You never knew, and I'm pretty sure that's why Dad preferred the traps.

I did not know it then, when as a child I watched my father wage war against pocket gophers, but this was excellent combat training for me, destined as I was to garden on the sand plain. Pocket gophers did well in Roseville's loamy soil, but sand is a virtual paradise for burrowing animals. It takes little effort to excavate a tunnel through light, sandy soil. The fine-textured particles are thrown up into airy mounds and the tunnel advances rapidly, yards and yards each day.

The first spring of gardening, I put a lot of effort into the asparagus bed. Asparagus roots take a long time to establish, but if done right an asparagus patch should last a long time, perhaps a lifetime. I laid out the bed with textbook precision. I dug trenches, brought in well-rotted turkey manure from the turkey farm north of town, and spread the spidery roots (expensive ones, Burpee's Best) twelve inches apart on little mounds of manure and soil. Lastly, I buried them and watered them well. Four years later, I could finally harvest the slender green stalks without fear of depleting the roots. Four years to wait before we could enjoy the king of vegetables. Four years before we glutted ourselves on bright green steamed asparagus, jade-colored stir-fried asparagus, asparagus in soups and risotto and soufflés.

One morning, to my dismay, a sandy dome appeared on the edge of the raspberries, and in no time at all—hours!—another popped up amid the asparagus. While I pondered what to do, the first asparagus root—one of only twelve—disappeared.

Panicky, I considered my options. There was the pan trap, but I couldn't imagine clubbing an animal to death. Besides, I wasn't sure they were still available or even legal. There was the Death Klutch—ugh! Nasty device. And there were poison peanuts. Well, what would you do? Like most female murderers in English mystery novels, I chose the passive-aggressive approach. I walked into the North Branch Mill and made my purchase.

In the short time it took me to act, I lost two more roots. That strengthened my resolve. Scoop in hand, I dug into the freshest mound and, not knowing whether I was doing it properly or effectively, slid several pellets into what I hoped was a runway, covering up my hole with a board, just like my father taught me. I stashed the canister of death away in a corner on the highest shelf above my workbench, feeling both anxious and guilty.

The poison pellets worked. The mounds stopped appearing. We dined on asparagus each spring for our remaining years in North Branch, but my pleasure in the vegetable faded.

My ambiguity toward pocket gophers is as deep and longstanding as my lessons in killing them. Even as I watched my father set traps, I was learning to love gophers by loving their nearest relatives. Pocket gophers are rodents, and from the time I was small I was drawn to this group of small mammals. Soft, silky woodland mice with great, dark eyes; sprightly, silly squirrels that finally—finally!—deigned our yard's trees large enough to live in; hyperactive chipmunks with their cunning little paws and pointed ears—these delighted me as a child and still delight me, even today. But it took me a long time to realize that I got visceral thrills whenever I saw them.

In my twenties, I enrolled in a mammology course at the University of Minnesota, taught by Dr. Elmer Birney, the young, ambitious curator of mammals for the University's natural history museum. It was an excellent, rigorous course with three hours of lecture per week and several hours of lab. I spent the lecture hours frantically scribbling notes in the dim half-light of a darkened lecture hall and the lab hours studying skulls.

An animal skull is a work of art, crafted by natural selection into perfect form. Each species' skull is unique, and the task in lab was to learn the distinctions so that we could, without a moment's hesitation, declare, "This is a red squirrel, *Tamiasciurus hudsonicus*," or "Aha! *Peromyscus maniculatus*, a white-footed mouse!" We held the beautiful, whitened skulls in our hands, turning them over and over, looking at bones—the eye orbitals, the rostrums, the mandibles holding the intricate teeth. I had marveled at complexity in ecosystems; in the skulls I saw this complexity on a smaller scale, carried around in every individual animal. The intricacy overwhelmed me. I loved the skulls.

It was through their skulls that I grew to love pocket gophers.

Pockets gophers are a distinctive group of rodents, and their bones reflect their burrowing life. The skulls are broad and robust, enabling them to plow through soil like an underground bulldozer. The zygomatic arch, a bone that protects the lower part of the eye, is sturdy and widened to anchor the well-developed jaw muscles. Like all rodents, they sport four large incisors, teeth prominent enough to earn them the nickname "Bucky." The front legs, used to push away dirt in tunnel construction, are thick and short. Gophers are burrowing machines, perfectly adapted to life underground, their bodies dedicated to excavation.

Pocket gophers are also an ancient group of mammals. The earliest fossil pocket gopher skulls are about 25 million years old. At the time they first appear in the fossil record, in the Miocene Epoch, North America was in a period of dryness, when vast stretches of grasslands covered its continental expanse. I think of the Miocene as a prairie time in our geological past, a time when large numbers of different types of grazers—horses, pronghorns, and camels, for example—roamed the North American grasslands. The pocket gopher, small and unobtrusive even then, was also a grazer of sorts: an underground grazer, roaming around unseen, feasting on the parts of plants that grew into the soil.

We can only guess the role pocket gophers played in Miocene ecosystems, but we know now that they are influential, if unheralded, members of North America's present-day grasslands and savannas. Without question, they sculpted the savanna on which North Branch was built and affected the other plants and animals that formed that biological community. The loose, sandy soil of the sand plain allowed pocket gophers to roam widely, throwing up fan-shaped mounds of dirt in their wanderings. These open patches of soil provided ideal spots for acorns to germinate and take root. Competition for water and sunlight, so fierce among prairie grasses, was lessened on the mounds, and they became nurseries for bur oaks and other woody species. Pocket gophers also affected, and still affect today, the well-being of established trees and shrubs. Given as they are to dining on roots, pocket gophers can severely prune back root systems of oaks, sand plums, hazel, and other savanna species. Sand plain oaks in some areas are dwarfish, stunted by the lack of root support and an inability to garner the necessary nutrients from the soil.

The pocket gopher in my area is known scientifically as *Geomys bursarius*, "Geo-mys," the earth mouse. It's a sweet, simple name for a shy, low-profiled animal, living out its life in the cool, dark soil under our feet.

The pocket gopher that invaded my asparagus bed was, perhaps, a descendent of the one who, a hundred years ago, launched the bur oaks in my yard, the oaks that give me such pleasure. How could I repay such kindness (however unwitting) by dishing out poison peanuts?

Well, the truth was, I couldn't. I poked the poison peanuts down the tunnel only once, and then my ambivalence got the best of me. The canister remained on the shelf over my workbench for nearly a decade, until I relinquished it in a household hazardous waste collection. Armed with the technology and chemicals of civilized society, I could have had my way with the pocket gopher. But we are most human when we are humane.

For the Birds

BIRD WATCHING is often a wedge prying open a wider love of nature, and this is especially true for children. Children are intrigued by the robins that bob around the playground, by the chipping sparrows that nest at eye-level in garden shrubbery. Birds are everywhere—on the local pond, in the mall parking lot, at the backyard bird feeder—and a conversation about "robin redbreast" or "ducky lucky" might lead into migration, or nesting behavior, or perhaps the food chain.

I have been a bird watcher for as long as I can remember. My parents gave me a small pocket guide with bright pictures for my seventh birthday, not to nudge me into a new pastime but to encourage an interest that was already full blown. Since then, I have worn out two additional guides and am working on my third. I carry my binoculars wherever I go, just in case I run into something interesting. Birds are striking and beautiful. Birds are subtle and graceful. There are so many different ways to know a bird—by its plumage, by its silhouette, by its song, by its characteristic movement—that my knowledge of it can never be complete. For most enthusiasts, birds provide a lifelong passion.

Each May I lead a four-day mini-course in bird watching at our local middle school. Aimed at eleven- to fourteen-year-olds, the course introduces students to different bird habitats and to the tools of the trade: binoculars and an identification guide. Each morning we spend two hours in the field getting acquainted with the art and science of bird watching. The course is called "For the Birds"—an attempt at humor, but a title that, alas, echoes some middle schoolers' sentiments exactly. Each year, the class roster is a mixed bag of students: some eager, some indifferent, some (those whose guidance counselors have signed them up) downright bored. But passion can be contagious.

One May morning I entered the middle school with binoculars slung around my neck, set to meet my new class. Only five girls had signed up for the course. I recognized one—her mother was a friend of mine, a fellow bird watcher. Two others turned innocent blue eyes toward me, wondering what would happen next. And two, with blond heads huddled together, whispered continuously.

I laid out expectations: this was an Outdoor Class. We'd be outside every morning, rain or shine, so come prepared! If it looked like rain, bring a poncho. We'd be keeping a list of the neat birds we saw, so we'd need a secretary. Any volunteers?

An outdoor class was a new concept. "Seriously," their skeptical eyes told me, "no one ever wore a raincoat." Or boots. Nevertheless, Gari Jo, one of the blue-eyed innocents, volunteered to record our sightings and took charge of the clipboard.

Next came the blue-covered copies of *Birds of North America*. We thumbed through the first few pages together, and I showed them the table of contents, the index, and page 202, a summary of the scientific families of perching birds. We talked a bit about perching birds. Better known as songbirds, these birds have feet evolved for grasping branches, three toes facing forward and one behind. All the students, even the whisperers, had a general idea of the difference between a songbird and a duck. This would come in handy.

Over the years, I have found that the biggest hurdle beginning bird watchers face in learning to identify an unfamiliar bird is trying to locate its picture amid a field guide's myriad possibilities. *Birds of North America* is not the preferred guide for most serious bird watchers, but it has a nice layout for teaching purposes. In general, water birds are found in the first half of the guide; land birds, the second. Maps showing where the birds live in summer and in winter are placed right next to pictures of the birds, so beginners can tell immediately whether the bird they're looking at is a likely possibility. And the large order of perching birds is introduced by a summary that describes salient characteristics of the scientific families—swallows swoop, catching insects in flight, wrens scold and have cocked tails; starlings group in noisy flocks; and so forth. If in the next four days the girls could begin thinking in terms of bird groupings, they would be able to locate unidentified birds in the future, thereby extending their knowledge beyond the mini-course.

Everyone grabbed a pair of binoculars and crowded out the door and into the waiting van. We headed for Wild River State Park's nature center and its well-tended bird feeding area. The girls would be inside for an hour, in a type of "observational blind," where we could talk about what we were seeing. The park's bird feeders, located with a sunny southern exposure, were in a grove of mature oaks. In mid-May, the oaks, decked out in dripping catkins, were a natural attractant for birds, and the feeders drew in additional species. It usually teemed with feathered life.

But not that particular week. In the days preceding our visit, a marauding black bear had trashed the feeders several nights running, and the naturalist had temporarily stopped stocking the feeders. Nevertheless (and lucky for us), some die-hard feeder visitors continued to hang around.

A flash of black and white landed in a nearby oak. General excitement swept through the class as several called out, "A woodpecker!"

"Is it a perching bird?" I asked.

"Yes!" they replied

"Well, not woodpeckers. They're in a separate group." We talked about what distinguished a woodpecker, and I pointed out the feet, two toes pointing forward and two behind. We located the wood-pecker family in the guide, and after much discussion the girls agreed it was bigger than a downy. *Hairy Woodpecker*, Gari Jo recorded.

We turned our attention to other small birds that seemed to pose on the rim of the empty feeders. These were true perching birds. We found their pictures on page 202, and I pointed out one's head-first movement down the tree trunk and another's striking black-and-white head pattern. Soon, *White-breasted Nuthatch* and *Black-capped Chickadee* made the list.

Having exhausted the birds in the feeding area, the girls de-cided to try their new skills outdoors at a nearby marsh. On the edge of the cattails, Laura exclaimed, "I see a bird! I see a bird! It's black and has red on its wings!"

"Is it a perching bird?" I asked.

"Yes!" They were certain.

"Let's find it!" I told them. "Page 202!"

Three of the girls paged rapidly to the perching bird section. Page 202 had a picture of the very bird under discussion. "Ooh! Ooh! Here it is!" Their excitement was genuine.

The whisperers, whose binoculars adorned their necks like pendants, rolled their eyes. They had yet to focus in.

By the end of the class we had listed sixteen birds, including a sora that had whinnied from the reeds. As we clambered into the van for the ride back to school, Gari Jo took a final peek at the red-winged blackbird strutting his stuff on his cattail perch. "Who ever thought bird watching could be this much fun?" she asked, of no one in particular.

The next morning, the birds sang brightly and the day sparkled with promise as we left the school grounds. We were destined for an abandoned pasture thick with shrubby growth. Bordered by a lake on one side and a small wood lot on another, this spot always yielded a plethora of birds. As we disembarked the van, a cacophony of song met our ears.

A pair of gray, robin-sized birds perched prominently on bare branches extending over the water. I pointed them out and asked if anyone noticed an interesting field mark.

The binoculars focused.

"They've got a white edge on their tails," Cassandra observed.

"Okay, good," I said. "Watch how they fly a short distance over the water and return to the same branch. What do you think they're doing?"

"Catching bugs?" Laura guessed.

"Yes! They're flycatchers. That's typical flycatcher behavior. Let's see if we can find them in the field guide."

The white band on the tail was a good clue. *Eastern Kingbird*, the girls decided. *Herring Gull*, *Common Yellowthroat*, and *Baltimore Oriole* made the list in quick succession. A pheasant crowed in the distance. Number twenty-one! Twenty-one species on the list, and we had not yet made our way into the meadow. I promised the class cocoa at the Rainbow Café in town if we extended the list to thirty birds that morning.

Incentive. We located a catbird meowing in a chokecherry bush, the girls giggling at its maniacal mimicry. We picked up a few woodland species in the trees, then spied a rose-breasted grosbeak that warbled high in a dead cottonwood. It didn't look like we'd make thirty species when one of the whisperers shrieked, "An eagle! An eagle!"

Six necks craned as a mature bald eagle, snowy head flashing, swooped low overhead, its talons clutching nesting materials of grass and sticks. We located the bald eagle's picture in the guide, where it was grouped with the hawks and vultures, but everyone could identify an eagle. Its magnificent size impressed even the reluctant bird watchers. Number thirty. Time for cocoa.

. . . .

Day three of the mini-course dawned cool and gray. After such wonderful birding the day before, it was hard to envision an encore. Light conditions are not as good and the birds perhaps a bit less active in cloudy weather, so I planned a visit to the Carlos Avery Wildlife Refuge. We would check out the ponds for waterfowl, then stop at a patch of savanna to look for prairie birds. There wasn't a peep from any student as they loaded up the van. Since the first morning, they had wisely dressed in jeans and old tennis shoes (no capri pants or exposed midriffs), and several even wore hooded sweatshirts—a departure from the dictates of middle-school fashion.

The Carlos Avery ponds yielded only resident birds. A family of wood ducks—mom, dad, and kids—paddled about, and, of course, there were mallards. Spring drakes are beautiful in their breeding plumage, and the girls thought the wood duck, in his iridescent greens and rusts, sporting the original ducktail hairdo, too exotic for a midwestern marsh. Two great blue herons stalked the edges of the cattails, but it was perhaps too late in the spring for interesting migrants passing through to the far north.

Alas, the savanna was worse, a disaster. An early hatch of mosquitoes had appeared over the weekend, and the insects hung in clouds around us. Even more alarming to the girls were the wood ticks, ambushing them from the dried grasses brushing the path, and the poison ivy, growing luxuriantly on the savanna's sand. The class tiptoed, knock-kneed, along the path, trying to avoid poison ivy on one side, persistent wood ticks on the other. Good sports, all of them, they had tucked their pants legs into their socks to keep the wood ticks from crawling on their skin—but not surprisingly, with a triple plague of mosquitoes, wood ticks, and poison ivy, no one was interested in birds. We headed back to the van for mid-morning treats of orange juice and doughnuts.

We tried one more marsh on the way back to school, staying in the van to finish the snack while we watched a pair of mallards. An elegant great egret patrolled the shallow water. It was while we had our binoculars trained on its rangy white form that the morning's true find appeared. In the background, behind the egret, a large, dark hawk landed, clutching a small rodent in its talons, and began *its* midmorning snack. Not a red-tailed hawk, and too small for an eagle. We paged through the guide to identify a rough-legged hawk, not an everyday sight in Chisago County. Gray days can be full of surprises.

On our last morning together, the girls and I were tired. The novelty of mini-courses had worn off, and the intensity of two-hour class periods had taken its toll. We headed for the St. Croix River Valley, where a dramatic bird, the turkey vulture, might be spotted soaring above the river. Only one girl of the five had been to the dalles of the St. Croix River, even though all of them lived within twenty miles of the gorge. The striking basalt cliffs form a deep, narrow valley, a landscape unlike any other in Minnesota. Even if the fervor of bird watching had lessened, the valley would be something to experience.

We spent a short time strolling around a neatly mowed picnic area, picking up a red-eyed vireo and a house wren for our list. Then, the girls wanted to play on the rocks, exploring the kettles and potholes, the famous geologic features of the dalles. Laura, the girl acquainted with the area, knew of a cave that made "the perfect house." They were, after all, only sixth-graders, despite their cool attitudes and hip fashions. Shouts of girlish laughter rang out in the fresh air as rough-winged swallows twittered about, swooping and darting over the river. The birds were catching insects for their nestlings. They were tending the next generation.

A Legacy of Water

ON A CLEAR JANUARY DAY, I ski on the North Branch golf course behind my house. The air is cold: the temperature has not yet risen to zero degrees, and the sky reverberates with blueness, like the clear ringing tone of a bell. The snow squeaks beneath the pressure of my skis, and my breath billows out from behind my scarf.

North Branch's golf course is flatter than flat, and it is possible to pick up speed as I slide my skis along a straight-away. Only a few of the well-tended greens are contoured with small manmade hillocks. When my children were young, they used these trifling artificial banks as sliding hills because the town has no natural slopes.

The older part of the course is shaded by craggy old bur oaks, their shadows etched in indigo across the snow's dazzling whiteness. An 1888 plat map labels this section of the course as a "driving park"—I think of fast horses and dashing young men. If you know where to look, remains of the track can be found on the first and ninth fairways.

A small creek—actually, a ditch that was dug a century ago to drain the marshy land—wanders across the eastern end of the course, forming a water hazard for several holes. It has no name, although a veteran golfer once told me, somewhat darkly, "It's been called many things." As I pass over on a footbridge, I see that ice has formed on its surface. A thin shelf of lacy filigree extends from bank to bank. Beneath, a dark ribbon of water beats like a pulse.

On this winter day, the water surrounding me is in its frozen state, save for the thin trickle of the creek. Even my breath, moist from my lungs, condenses into frost on my scarf and the strands of hair escaping my hat. The snow seems static, even harmless, no more than white fluff. Yet water in all its various forms has crafted the landscape on which I ski. Always dynamic, it has been a ponderous, undeniable force on the surface of the earth.

Minnesotans live in intimate relationship with the legacies of one fascinating manifestation of water: glaciers. In the Pleistocene Age, the most recent one million years of geologic time, glaciers moved over the northern half of North America. Minnesotans received a multitude of gifts from these great sheets of ice: our cherished lakes, numbering more than 15,000; our rivers and streams, formed from the melt waters; and the very topography we traverse each day.

The glaciers have given us an interior landscape as well. They affect how we think about Time, their presence marking a punctuation point in the flow of history. When I think of Minnesota history, Time begins with the rolling back of the enormous ice sheets. I conjure up images of icy water trickling through immense mounds of rock and rubble. I imagine invasion by cold-hardy plants, the blossoming of a biotic community, a slow build-up of soil, and the gradual appearance of the forests and grasslands so familiar to our visions of Minnesota.

Time existed before the glaciers, of course. Lake Superior's basin and the North Shore's beloved basalt formations took shape long before the Ice Age, as did the golden sandstone cliffs rising above the Mississippi River. Yet all that graces our interior landscape, our inward perception of Minnesota—the lakes and rivers, the hills and valleys, even the rocks, rubble, and sand that gave rise to our soils—is a direct consequence of the last glacier that edged its way across what is now Minnesota sometime earlier than 34,000 years ago.

Glaciers are born when the climate cools. Snow fails to melt in summer and survives into the following winter. Snowflakes become compact. They may melt and refreeze into an icy mass. If summer's warmth does not melt the winter snow over a long period of time, the mass accumulates and forms a glacier. The large accumulation of ice is tremendously heavy and begins to move under the pressure of its own weight. Everything about a glacier seems larger than life. Its depth can be thousands of feet. Imagine an ice mass one mile high: Minnesota's glaciers are thought to have been this tall. The weight of so much ice actually depresses the land over which it moves. When a glacier recedes, the earth rebounds and increases in elevation. This effect sometimes reverses the directional flow of rivers because, of course, water flows downhill.

In the last one million years, there have been four periods of North American glaciation. Each advancing ice sheet eradicated most of the imprint of the previous ones, so the glacial age we know most fully is the last one. That event, the Wisconsin glaciation, formed Minnesota's present topography. The popular image of the Ice Age is of one monolithic ice sheet, but actually several fingers, or lobes, of ice extended from one massive sheet in Canada east of the Rockies. These lobes invaded Minnesota from different northerly directions. They advanced and retreated several times, leaving behind piles of rocky till (moraines) at their leading and lateral edges and creating marshy lowlands and lakes.

Chisago County bears the lasting marks of two of these glacial advances. One advance, termed the Superior lobe, came out of Lake Superior's basin from the northeast, pushing ground-up rock and rubble as it moved forward. As in all glaciers, additional material is carried along with the ice flow in a motion geologists liken to that of a conveyor belt. Rocks, gravel, sand—even bits of wood from unfortunate trees in the advancing glacier's path—are moved along and carried to the edge of the ice.

Snow and ice are needed to keep a glacial ice mass moving. The supply is abundant as the climate continues to cool. However, each glacial interval ended with a gradual warming of yearly temperatures. When the melting rate of the Superior lobe at its terminus equaled the flow rate outward from the thickest part of the sheet, the glacier stalled. In its retreat it left behind mounds of rock and rubble and piles of sand and gravel that powerful streams under the glacier had delivered to the edge of the ice. Two northern suburbs of the Twin Cities take their names from these moraine features: Mounds View and Arden Hills.

When it retreated, the Superior lobe vacated an elongate, oval depression in the underlying bedrock that had existed long before the glaciers. This depression, called the Stacy basin, caught water pooling from the melting ice and became the basis for the first of several glacial lakes in the Chisago region, Glacial Lake Lind.

As the glaciers melted, glacial lakes became a common feature in prehistoric Minnesota. Imagine the tremendous volume of water released by melting ice masses thousands of feet high. Even today, after a winter of heavy snowfall, sheets of water collect in the shallowest of basins. The glacial melt water pooled into gargantuan bodies of water, the largest, Lake Agassiz, extending from the northwest corner of the state far into Canada, its volume once greater than all five present-day Great Lakes combined. But many smaller glacial lakes that are seldom mentioned are, nonetheless, noteworthy.

Glacial Lake Lind was long and narrow, about thirty miles in length and eight miles in breadth, and existed for about a thousand years. It met its end not through drainage but by in-fill with sand carried in melt water from the retreating Superior lobe. It left its mark on Chisago County in the form of iron-rich reddish clay and silt layers that are exposed in certain parts of the area. The red color, usually indicating the presence of iron, links Chisago County to the iron deposits in northern Wisconsin and the rosy sandstone cliffs of the Bayfield peninsula.

The second glacial advance to sculpt Chisago County gathered momentum as the Superior lobe was retreating. To the west of the Superior lobe, a second finger of ice, known as the Des Moines lobe, extended out of Canada and as far south as central Iowa. This massive ice sheet spawned an offshoot that moved in a northeast direction from the Minneapolis/St. Paul region into present-day Chisago County. The offshoot, termed the Grantsburg sublobe, advanced very quickly, moving at an estimated three to seven kilometers—or about two miles—per year, a rate of flow researchers term a "surge." It eventually came to a standstill just north of where the present St. Croix River bends outward and forms the little bump in Minnesota's east-central border.

As the Grantsburg sublobe retreated, melting water flowed off the diminishing ice sheet, carrying with it finely ground sand, which it deposited over the land recently scoured by the Superior lobe and watered by Lake Lind. The sand accumulated in vast amounts, fifty or more feet deep. It covered a large portion of the Stacy basin, layering over the rock and rubble left behind by both glacial lobes. Only a few especially big mounds of glacial till poked up beyond the sand. The most prominent one rises east of North Branch near the town of Sunrise: Amador Hill.

Somewhat later, the flowing water was dammed for a time and pooled into another lake, Glacial Lake Anoka. Wave action by the lake shifted the sand back and forth, smoothing the surface and forming the broad, flat landscape that we call the Anoka Sand Plain.

As I ski over the North Branch golf course, I try to imagine a shimmering lake, its blue water glinting under the noonday sun. My skis retrace the caress of the waves that molded the land's contours.

Snow and ice and flowing water form the past and present features of this sparkling winter world. Soon I finish the track that loops the course. I snap off my skis and look out over the snow-covered fairway. Glacial Lake Anoka was huge—well over forty miles in length and wider than Glacial Lake Lind had been. It would have dwarfed present-day Lake Mille Lacs or the combined Upper and Lower Red Lakes, our representative examples of very big lakes. Afloat on Lake Anoka in a rowboat and anchored over the patch of lake bed that is now my backyard, I would not have been able to see the far shore. Broad like Mille Lacs, the lake would have been fearsome in a storm. On a frigid January day, its frozen expanse would have yawned in all directions, snow crystals catching the sunlight like diamonds, each kin to the massive glaciers that once ruled the north.

When the glacial lake was gone, all that remained was its bed. It is an odd feeling, residing in a lake bed, and I often forget that I do. Yet, now and then, the cryptic lake bed appears to remind me.

On a cold April morning, construction workers are excavating water and sewer lines to "improve" Oak Street. The sixty-year-old lines, running six feet below the surface, are being replaced and a badly needed storm sewer added. At noon, the project's general contractor, knowing my interest, knocks on my door. The lines are exposed—would I care to take a look?

Outside, peering into the hole, I view a startling sight: the soil is dramatically layered. The first eighteen inches or so consist of fine, taupe-colored particles. This is nothing new—it is the familiar soil that I sift through my fingers when I work in the garden. But directly beneath the top layer is a three-foot band of pure white sand. It sparkles brilliantly in the sunlight. Nothing sullies its uniform color or texture. It looks virginal, primeval. It looks . . . like it belongs in a lake bed. Beneath the white sand is a third layer, darker and less uniform in color. At the bottom of the hole are the pipes, uncovered for the first time in sixty years. Who knows what lies beneath them? Six feet down and there is no bedrock in sight.

Like many natural occurrences, the hole requires interpretation. The layers are known collectively as the soil profile and when analyzed provide a visual history of North Branch's recent geologic past.

The top layer, the taupe-colored soil, has formed since the glacial lakes dried up and vegetation moved in to colonize the newly open area. In the ten thousand or so years since the last lake disappeared, plants took root, grew, and died. Their leaves and stems decayed and mixed with the sand to gradually form a sandy soil—the soil that nurtured the famous potatoes a mere century ago. The general contractor, who had seen many holes and many soil profiles, remarked that this first soil layer was unusually thick. In some areas he had excavated, the soil was much thinner, eroded by wind or water.

Since our street abutted the first platting of North Branch, the soil under Oak Street's pavement was probably never cultivated. We know that the open land beyond the platted town where Oak Street now runs was used as a common pasture and, of course, as a "driving park." These eighteen inches of soil accumulated over thousands of years. In the past 130 years, however, since the sod of the prairie grasses was opened and plowed, wind or rain has eroded measurable inches of the fine, light soil. Because people do not know how to make soil but instead rely on the processes of time and ecosystems for it, this is a resource that not only has been used but also is in danger of disappearing.

The next layer, the white sand, is exactly what it looks like: unadulterated outwash from the glacier's melt water, the lake bed of Glacial Lake Anoka. Geologists have characterized the sand as "very pure grayish quartz." Its thickness in different locations of the sand plain varies. In North Branch, it is generally fifteen to twenty feet thick but can be as deep as fifty feet. Sand plain farmers refer to the white sand as "sugar sand" because by its appearance and its texture—exactly the particle size of sugar crystals—you might be tempted to spoon it on your morning cereal. To water their gardens, many folks in the North Branch area have a shallow sand-point well that taps into this layer.

The third layer, which I didn't get as close a peek at, may well have been the glacial till of the Grantsburg sublobe. This glacial deposit, though mostly obscured by sand, is revealed in some areas. Gray, with the consistency of clay, it holds water well.

Having seen what is beneath the surface, I now understand better what goes on above it. I can fully appreciate why I need to water my garden every other day when it doesn't rain—water from the sprinkler trickles through eighteen inches of sandy soil and then into sand which quickly drains it away. The puddles that form on the golf course after a terrific downpour take on new meaning, too, demonstrating that the sand layer must be completely saturated.

Ice and snow, lakes and sand—commonplace materials that change the face of the earth.

Earth Day Lessons

ONE OF THE JOYS of living in a smaller community is being able to walk about town. Our neighborhood was a wonderful teacher, and my children and I learned a great deal about our home in North Branch on our daily treks to school. Our route took us down Oak Street past the medical clinic and our neighbors' homes, over to Maple Street and across the golf course's creek to the county road fronting the elementary school. We walked in all types of weather—the chilly rains of September, the spare, frosty mornings of November before permanent snow, the pleasant May mornings just before school let out for the summer. As long as there wasn't an electrical storm or temperatures of negative forty degrees, we walked.

At a slow pace, we took in the world. We absorbed the scent of bur oaks and front lawns, of old wood and aging asphalt. We watched certain trees keep pace with the calendar. Mrs. Pederson's sugar maple on the corner of Sixth and Maple was an early harbinger of change—the first to turn red in the fall, the first to stand naked in the cold October air. On inclement mornings, the Sausens' cedar tree near Fourth and Maple harbored interesting birds, seeking shelter and hanging out at the family's bird feeder.

The golf course creek ran through their property. The children and I watched the little stream as winter approached, keeping an eye on the ice as it formed along the banks, first lacy and delicate, then extending outward as shelves along the edges. The running water cut away at this ice as it formed and reformed until, during a cold snap of subzero weather, the ice won out. The creek then became a slender ribbon of ice, winding from the golf course, through the Sausens' backyard, under Highway 14, and past the Alvin place until it hooked up with the north branch of the Sunrise River a few blocks away. The Sunrise emptied into the St. Croix, a federally designated Wild and Scenic River ten miles east of town. The St. Croix rushed headlong southward to join with the Mississippi at Hastings, Minnesota; and the mighty Mississippi, after draining the mid–North American continent, released its water into the Gulf of Mexico. All the water leaking out of Chisago County's high water table, the water we watched on our way to school, eventually found its way to the ocean. The children and I talked about this as we paused by the creek. It was a good way to teach geography and our connection to far-off places. In this way, Andy, Katie, and I took in the world as we walked to school.

One cool, drippy April morning, the children and I walked down Oak Street, alert for signs of spring. Although March had teased us with a few days of warm, dry air, April had brought us—well, April weather: cold, rainy, fickle at best. The lawns were greening in the rain, and sprightly, elf-like crocuses poked through the soil in some gardens. But the gnarled and cranky bur oaks looming overhead did not seem to have a clue about spring. While maple and elm buds swelled on branches, the oaks appeared stuck in the recesses of February, impervious to the lengthening days and warming air.

A shower the night before had brought earthworms to the

surface. They were scattered across the road like strands of flesh-colored spaghetti. Andy, a second-grader, was concerned—obsessed—about the welfare of the worms. His teacher that year, Mrs. Peterson, loved science, and Andy had spent hours reading books on different kinds of rocks, on the solar system and space travel, on animals and their habitats. Under her enthusiastic tutelage, he had become enraptured with raptors, producing finely drawn pencil sketches of hawks and falcons with hooded eyes and ferocious talons.

As Earth Day approached, Mrs. Peterson turned her class's attention to ecology. Andy was now tuned in to worms and the role they played in the ecosystem. As we made our way down the damp, puddle-pocked street, he chattered on and on about how they chewed up the dead leaves, turning them into soil; how they wiggled through the dirt, creating air tunnels so the plant roots can "breathe." He was earnestly concerned that we not step on any. Little Katie, a kindergartner, took Andy's worm lecture to heart. Conscientious to a fault, she minced down Oak Street with baby steps, watching her feet.

It was a lovely spring morning, the air heavy with mist. Water droplets hung from the tips of evergreen needles and lined the furrows of the oaks' bark. The visibility was so shortened that it felt as if God had clamped a large bowl over North Branch, making the universe very small, the edges of the bowl no more than two blocks away in any direction. Bands of migrating robins, newly arrived, patrolled the lawns.

Halfway down Maple Street, as we approached the creek, I noticed that the yard across the street from the Sausens, bordering the creek on its west bank, had odd little signs marking its perimeter. The signs were green and white, about four inches square, held a foot off the ground by black plastic stakes. The writing on the cards was too small to make out from a distance, except for the top line, which read, "ChemLawn." I crossed Maple for a better look. The yard, it seemed, had been sprayed the day before. Small children and pets were to be kept off the lawn for the following two days. There was a date—4/18—scribbled at the bottom of the warning sign, presumably indicating the day the lawn was treated.

Apparently, some neighbors were in pursuit of the Perfect Lawn. Perfect Lawns are those fertilized by phosphorus and nitrogen, water-soluble elements that run freely into lakes and streams on rainy days. Perfect Lawns are dosed with herbicides to rid the yard of any plants that would mar an emerald carpet of grass. But Perfect Lawns are perfect only for cultivated grass. For children, pets, and birds, they can be deadly. Male robins, famished after migration, red breasts puffed out from the cold, hopped past the green and white signs. They pulled worms out of the treated lawn and gobbled them with gusto.

I have tried to be prudent in speaking my mind publicly to the greater world. For example, I have for years resisted writing a letter decrying the burning of fall leaves in town— literally a health issue—because I fear the inevitable headlines: "Leaf Burned over Burning Leaves." But this seemed pretty clear to me, so I wrote a letter to the *North Branch Post Review*, decrying the harm to children and animals. The letter appeared in the paper's next edition.

There was a double irony in the appearance of the green and white signs. Not only had they popped up in conjunction with Earth Day, but the Perfect Lawn itself didn't look any different from the other lawns in town. North Branch is built on a sand plain. The soil is *sandy*. We could not negate that fact, not with sod, not with fertilizer, not with herbicides running off into the creek. None of our lawns would ever be featured in *Better Homes and Gardens*.

The day after my letter appeared in the *Post Review*, I happened to stroll past the medical clinic, where Tom worked. To my amazement, *its* lawn had sprouted little green and white signs. They were lined up like smartly square soldiers, every five feet, along the curb bordering the street. I stared, bewildered. Was this someone's idea of a practical joke? I hadn't expected any public reaction to my letter. Rattled, I yanked the signs and cradled them in my arms like a ChemLawn bouquet, thinking I'd throw them away

When I got them back to the house, however, I saw that the signs were dated like the Maple Street signs, but later. They were not the same signs I had seen the week before and, in fact, had nothing to do with my letter in the newspaper. I had jumped to the wrong conclusion. Apparently, Chisago Health Services, the owner of the clinic, was also pursuing a Perfect Lawn. Chisago Health Services—the keeper of our community's health, my husband's employer, the corporation that wrote his paycheck every two weeks.

My ChemLawn bouquet embarrassed me, and I began to see it as an emblem of a cautionary tale: none of us in our industrialized world can claim to have clean hands. This truth was my personal Earth Day lesson, and it sobered me.

There is a second lesson, though, that we have yet to master: while we applaud the Mrs. Petersons who teach ecology, we fail to put ourselves in the curriculum. The vigor of the robins, the purity of the creek, the vitality of the earthworms—what we do affects them. They are shared responsibility.

This Earth Day lesson remains: the web of life connects us all.

Three

Righting the Right of Way

IN 1860, a person standing on the hill behind the state capitol in St. Paul and facing north would front a largely pristine wilderness. The capital city already boasted ten thousand residents, a commanding state house with gleaming dome and pillars, and a bustling, if somewhat ragtag, urban area. But to the north, beyond the reach of major waterways, lay untouched oak savanna, miles of marsh and tamarack swamp, and rich pine forests too far from the St. Croix River and its tributaries to be profitably cut. Lake Superior, offering a potentially rich fishing industry and a link to eastern cities, was remote. The 1860 census recorded a cluster of rough dwellings and a population of eighty souls eking a living off the rocky hillside at Duluth.

In colonial times, people traversed the wilderness on foot, by horse, or with wagons. But by 1860, railroads crisscrossed the eastern United States, and Minnesotans clamored for this high-tech solution to their transportation difficulties. The first railroad in the new state was built in 1862, between the capital city and St. Anthony (later known as Minneapolis). Two years later, that same line extended to Anoka, and then to St. Cloud. Lines west to Breckenridge, southwest to St. Peter, and south to the Iowa border soon followed.

A railroad linking the Twin Cities and Lake Superior had been envisioned since before statehood, but making it a reality required money. State and federal land grants gave a boost to the project, and St. Paul's city council, led by local banker William Banning, issued municipal bonds to subsidize the endeavor. Banning enlisted the support of an outsider, Philadelphia financier Jay Cooke, and encouraged him to also invest in the rich pinelands through which the line would run. Cooke did so, appearing in 1868 dressed in "top hat, cloth shoes, long coat, colored waistcoat, gold watch-chain and stick" to inspect his investment. He paddled a canoe on Lake Superior to evaluate the potential for a harbor. Duluth at the time had twenty buildings.

Cooke and Banning's line, the Lake Superior and Mississippi Railroad, was completed in 1870. The work was accomplished in stages, rails reaching Wyoming by 1868 and North Branch shortly thereafter. Steam engines required water, and the railroad builders positioned stations at points where the line crossed a water source. North Branch Station was sited on the north branch of the Sunrise River. The town was platted in 1870, and the station received a post office from the U.S. government later that fall. The presence of an official post office gave the community an air of stability, and several businesses moved in.

North Branch owed its life to the Lake Superior and Mississippi Railroad in the same way the heart is dependent upon the blood flowing through it. Goods came into town and products shipped out of town via the rail. From the very beginning, North Branch was linked to the wider world and shared a common destiny with it. By 1894, North Branch's railroad had joined the empire of James J. Hill, becoming part of the Great Northern Railroad. Subsequent mergers transformed it into the Northern Pacific and, later still, the Burlington Northern Railroad, the name it retained in 1984 when we moved to town.

Despite the fact that it thundered through town several times a day, rattling teacups and shaking the floorboards of our house, we came to appreciate the train. As I heard its roar, I felt linked to Lake Superior, our most recent home, and also to St. Paul, my childhood city. Although I felt a vague thrill of terror every time I drove over the crossing, especially when I had a baby along, strapped into a car seat, I knew the train embodied vigorous life.

Trains didn't always pass us by, either. They often stopped at the mill, just north of the main intersection, to pick up grain. At the crossing, the red lights would flash, the black-and-white arms would descend, and the highway in all directions would clog with autos as linemen coupled and uncoupled dusty gray grain cars. The thuds and clanks that rang out told us that North Branch was a working town, connected to the world of commerce.

What we really enjoyed about living close to the tracks, however, was not the train itself but the railroad right of way, the corridor of land through which the tracks ran. On late spring evenings, when we knew a train was not coming, Tom and I would take our children for walks along the tracks, heading south out of town. In the golden light and lengthening shadows of mild May evenings, we'd scuffle through the dried remains of the prairie grass that grew untended on either side of the track. We had experience with railroad rights of way from a former home in southern Minnesota, and we knew they contained some of the last prairie plants in the state, indeed, the last remnants of prairie in North America. Since track had been laid over untouched land, rights of way had never been plowed or cultivated. Furthermore, rights of way had been periodically subjected to fire, ignited by sparks from wheels grinding on the steel rails. The flames preserved the fire-adapted prairie plants within the railroad corridor long after land beyond it had been converted to farm fields, towns, and suburbs. These plants were the descendents of those—or were even, possibly, the same plants—that had thrived when the railroad first penetrated the wild savanna. A slender ribbon of North Branch's past flanked the railroad tracks.

Along the Burlington Northern line running through town, we identified the three dominant grasses that marked the native savanna. In the fall, when these grasses were at full height, we'd admire the tall, gangly big bluestem, waving awkwardly in the wind; the more graceful, amber-colored Indian grass; and, my favorite, the thick, downy bunches of little bluestem, growing in wine-colored tufts with seed heads of soft, fluffy awns.

On our spring walks, we searched for the delicate, subtle spring prairie flowers we suspected were hiding out among the remains of dried grass. Right in town, half a block from our house, we discovered small bird's-foot violets, with dissected leaves resembling a crow's footprint. There, too, we found the lovely purple avens, nicknamed "prairie smoke." Crouching low to the ground, its magenta flowers resembled inverted jester's caps. As the flower matured, the long stamens grew to feathery plumes that waved in the wind and called to mind its nickname. Dark-hued spiderwort grew farther down the track in a low area; white prairie clover and pink, shrubby prairie roses bloomed in June. Tom and I craved contact with the natural world, but we also desired the convenience and community of living in town. The railroad right of way was our tiny piece of wildness.

I loved the wildness of the right of way, but I also loved how it enabled me to peer into the past.

The backyards abutting the right of way contained wonderful, old bur oak trees, dark, knotted, and craggy. The right of way itself had, of course, once harbored oaks, too, but these were cut down when the tracks were laid. Only the grasses remained, and when they were fully grown, in the fall, the tracks through the heart of town had both components of the original savanna: bur oaks and big bluestem grass.

On walks about town, I'd keep my eye on the oak/grass combination. As I retraced my route up Oak Street, I'd pause at the point where the road rose gently toward the tracks. Tilting my head, I would see if I could make the savanna appear. I'd lift up my chin until the paved surface of Oak dropped from view and squint my eyes to blur the Deming house behind the trees. Then, every time, the savanna would spring before my eyes: the silhouette of the oaks, the golden gawkiness of the bluestem. I could see how it must have been, before the town, before the railroad. For a moment, the savanna would be right there, and I would travel back in time to when the bur oaks—these same bur oaks that tower over Oak Street now—grew amidst miles and miles of grass.

Burlington Northern shut down the line running through North Branch in 1991. Freight shipped south by rail had reduced to a trickle that the Cambridge line could handle. The mill wished to retain the option of shipping grain to Duluth by rail, though, so the tracks on the north side of town were kept open, but the volume of their traffic also decreased. Now when a train chugged into North Branch, it was a slow, deliberate process, the cars backed carefully down the track from Rush City. For the first time ever, no trains roared through town. A smooth, continuous link with the town's earliest days, running through good times and bad, through the potato boom, the Great Depression, and two world wars, was suddenly severed.

The loss of the train was a blow to North Branch's sense of identity, but we did not wholly regret its demise. The crossings lost their terror. I no longer worried that the warning lights might not be functioning, and I realized that when my children began to drive, I would not have to worry about them, or their friends, playing "beat the train." We no longer had lengthy waits at the crossing while cars coupled and uncoupled.

But there was the issue of the unused track. All over the state, citizen groups had been transforming abandoned railroad lines into bike trails, with happy results. A local group formed to promote the idea, and after considerable effort convinced the Chisago

County Board of Commissioners to allow the line to be used as an all-purpose trail, accommodating both bicycles and snowmobiles. The county board was most concerned that the right of way be kept intact and not be sold off in tiny pieces to adjacent landowners, in the event that a light rail system might in the future come our way.

For the Bicycle Task Force, the decision to retain the right of way meant that a recreational trail could become a reality. Members of our local Audubon chapter, including Tom and me, advocated preserving the tiny patch of prairie/savanna that grew on the right of way. We wrote letters to the newspaper and spoke up at community meetings. Several Audubon members were influential on the Bicycle Task Force, and preserving the native vegetation became an important secondary reason to transform the abandoned right of way into a recreational trail.

Before work on the trail could begin, Burlington Northern had to dismantle the rails. One morning a crew appeared with a large, noisy machine built just for that purpose. It pulled up the heavy steel rails; then a second machine dislodged and carted off the creosote-soaked ties. It took several weeks, and when they were finished, a clear, open path led southward straight to the edge of the horizon. It would make a fine trail.

The next stage of dismantlement was less benign.

A few weeks later, on a soft, May day, heavy equipment rumbled onto the abandoned line. A massive front-end loader bumbled about, scooping up soil, gravel, and all other material on and near the bed, depositing it into an elongated dump truck. The earth was scraped clean, and the small prairie plants—the bird's-foot violet, the prairie smoke, the bluestem—which had survived 120 years of trains, were gone. We later learned that Burlington Northern had been reclaiming the crushed rock that formed the structural support of the roadbed to sell for profit.

Although the wild plants initially appeared devastated, after the dust had settled on the damage done by the front-end loader we saw that all was not lost. Though the plants along the rail bed in town had been wiped out, the right of way outside city limits extended sixty feet on either side of the former tracks and still supported native species. These could be preserved and might even seed into soil scarred by heavy equipment. There was reason to hope.

The effort to establish a bicycle trail continued. The energetic and perseverant Bicycle Task Force pursued funding through grants and federal programs. They sought the aid and advice of other groups that had successfully built trails, and they promoted their plan to local leaders in North Branch, Stacy, and Wyoming, the sand plain communities through which the trail would run. When the county board had given its blessing for the task force to pursue building the trail, I suspect the commissioners doubted it would ever come to pass. But the money for the trail came in, first in trickles, then in a steady flow. A half-million-dollar grant from the first Bush administration's Rails to Trails program assured that an eighteen-mile trail beginning in North Branch and running south to the border of Chisago County would be built.

While the serious, hard-working Bicycle Task Force labored to drum up funds, we Auduboners harbored a secret fantasy. Among ourselves, we dreamed of setting fire to the railroad corridor. It would be so satisfying to see it burn, we thought, like scratching a long-standing itch.

This fantasy was not a deviant form of pyromania. (At least, we didn't think so.) Rather, it was something the savanna/prairie needed. Although native plants grew on the right of way, nonnative weedy species had invaded. Foxtail, smooth brome, sweet clover—all of these were exotics that flourished in cultivated fields. Unlike native prairie species, these European invaders were sensitive to fire. One cleansing burn would eliminate them and encourage the natives to proliferate. We Auduboners joked about sneaking out on a dry, calm evening with a well-placed match, but we were too old, too sensible, and too law-abiding to carry out the scheme.

However, when we received an invitation from the Bicycle Task Force to enact our fantasy, we were utterly thrilled. Somehow, the task force had convinced the county board that burning the right of way was a good idea. They then enlisted the help of the local Department of Natural Resources office and the North Branch fire department. On a clear, calm evening in April, we gathered at the right of way in town, dressed in our grubbiest jeans and jackets, zealous glints in our eyes.

The DNR routinely carries out prescribed burns on state-owned prairie lands, and one of the department's employees directed us. He hauled out shovels, brooms, and acetylene torches. Some of us would set fires; others would stamp them out. We agreed we would switch positions every so often because, of course, everyone wanted to set fires.

April is an ideal time to burn a prairie. Native grasses are slow starters in the spring; in April, they have not yet begun to grow, and only the previous summer's dry remains will burn. However, the weedy non-natives have already sprouted and will be killed by the fire, reducing competition. The ash left over after a burn has an added fertilizing benefit, releasing nutrients into the soil for the soon-to-sprout prairie grasses. Prescribed burns merely mimic what spring grass fires have been doing for ages. In fact, the first people on Minnesota's savannas and prairies did exactly what we were going to do that night—deliberately set fire to revive the grass. The natives knew fire encouraged lush growth that attracted game—bison and deer—and they altered the vegetation to ensure a food supply. Fire also cleared out brush and made the savanna easier to traverse. Our evening's activity would echo the past as well as restore a future.

The conditions for burning were ideal that evening. There was not a breath of air, and it was not overly dry. The burn would be light and controllable. Nevertheless, the DNR man led us a block out of town before allowing us to light the torches.

With a small thrill of exhilaration we watched the first tiny flames lick the dried grass tufts and then fan out in an ever-widening arc, leaving scorched earth behind them. When the flames reached the bare path where the tracks had been, those bearing brooms gave the little tongues of fire a good whack, making sure they were dead. Shovel bearers used the same technique, but less effectively. They could also dig up dirt and smother the flames, but the burn proceeded at so leisurely a pace that such action wasn't necessary. There was a pecking order in the desirability of firefighting tool: acetylene torches were first, everyone preferring to do the damage; brooms were second, because they provided that satisfying w*hack*; shovels, those heavy, clunky implements, a distant third.

My exhilaration kindled when it came my turn to man the torch. I had never set fire to anything other than candles or campfires; there was a wildness to torching grass that sparked me. I ran exuberantly ahead of the brooms and shovels, lighting the land and leaving behind me clouds of black smoke billowing heavenward. The long yellow rays of the setting sun streaked the countryside and turned my skin golden. With cleansing fire, I was bringing back the prairie.

At about the three-mile mark outside of town, we were spent. The wind had picked up slightly, and several farmers appeared at the edges of their fields, looking somewhat askance, having no doubt seen the black cloud approaching from the north. We didn't want to risk a wayward fire or public disapproval. Sooty and satisfied, we climbed into the back of the DNR pickup that had followed behind us and rode it back to town, admiring our work. In the next six weeks, we would watch the prairie green up with lush, new growth.

The recreational trail extending from North Branch to the county line became a reality in 1996. It cost nearly a million dollars to pave the eighteen miles of trail, a small fortune raised solely from donations and grants. The task force named it the "Sunrise Prairie Trail," a pleasant, euphonious name, if not precisely accurate since it is not truly a prairie but a savanna and it at no time crosses the

Sunrise River. Still, the name conjures images of a wild place, of a past, of an inheritance, which the right of way surely is.

As predicted, large numbers of people use the trail. On summer evenings, when the air is sweet with the scent of growing crops, older couples stroll back and forth, young families hauling babies on bicycle carriers pedal out, and rollerbladers zip around, taking their exercise. Joggers use it, too, and so do neighbors walking their dogs.

It is poignant that North Branchers seek out this one remaining skinny strip of savanna in which to repose and recreate. It seems that wildness has something to offer us even when stripped of its vastness. And it is ironic, too, that the railroad, the first symbol of civilization to penetrate the wilderness, is now the last repository of it, reminding us that what appears to threaten us most may in truth be a source of our salvation.

Destruction

ON A FRIDAY IN JULY 1995, an approaching storm smudged the western horizon of North Branch with blue-black clouds. We had sweltered in the month's hot, humid weather. "Summer hangs heavy on us," I had written in my journal the week before. "The air wraps us like a warm, wet blanket, a smothering evening."

At the workweek's end, Tom toiled feverishly, trying to clear his desk of undictated medical charts. He wanted a free weekend with no trips to the clinic or hospital. The kids, languid from the heat, lounged in front of the television, waiting for dinner.

The garden had been producing bountifully, supplying us with lettuce, peapods, and raspberries for weeks already. Green beans and zucchini flaunted brightly colored blossoms, and tiny green tomatoes clung to the vines. Despite this homegrown wealth, I'd decided to run to Subway for sandwiches. In the oppressive heat, I couldn't imagine cooking in my small, airless kitchen. Besides, the children considered food not prepared by their mother to have a certain cachet. We could celebrate Katie's return from summer camp, Tom's impending weekend without call duty, and my success (however fleeting) in producing a clean house and five loads of wash in one day. But at six o'clock the darkening sky sent me scurrying to pick up dinner earlier than I had planned. I didn't want to be caught in the rain.

An hour later, just as we sat down to eat, the civil defense siren blew. The ear-splitting whine emanated from the city's Power and Water Company a block away. Firemen frequently sounded the siren for fires, but in this case the scream rose to a steady pitch and held constant for several minutes. Even our youngest child knew this as the unmistakable signal that a tornado had been spotted.

Despite meteorologists' cautions to the contrary, most Minnesotans do not snap to attention when the tornado siren blows. At least, I don't. I look to the sky. Our local whistles sound if a funnel has been sighted anywhere in the county. At times I've stood in my sunny backyard under a tornado warning, watching the Chisago Lakes area twelve miles to the south get battered by a storm. At other times, like the week before this storm, I have been outside, child in arms, watching funnel clouds roil overhead with nary a peep from the siren. While the siren gets our attention, we read the sky to see what it says.

On this Friday evening, it told us to be "alert!" We could see that the storm was still some way off, so we elected to finish our meal at the kitchen table. Even so, the very air had turned greenish. Lloyd Pearson's white house across the street had assumed an unnatural hue, and color electrified the grass. The radio on the countertop popped and snapped with static. Between the fuzzy, crackling noises, the announcer told us that the storm covered a large portion of central Minnesota. Funnels fingered the heavily populated counties of the Twin Cities to our south and extended west to Redwood Falls. But the storm was most intensely pummeling Isanti County, directly west of us. A tornado, on the ground for several minutes, had splintered numerous houses in a Cambridge neighborhood. North Branch lay in its direct path.

Dinner over, I walked out to the street for a better view of the approaching storm. Neighbors gathered to observe what we agreed must be a "wall cloud," a sullen blue thunderhead towering above us and encompassing the entire western horizon. Thunder rumbled continuously, ominously, on the breathless air, and white shafts of lightning pierced the atmosphere. This display and the pea-green light impressed the assembled neighbors. All in our forties, we told ourselves that we had never experienced anything like it, especially the constant thunder. When the lightning felt dangerous, we turned back to our houses. Tom and I took a last look at the now deserted street and went inside. The children and the edgy Shetland sheepdog waited for us in the basement.

We did not live elegantly in the basement at 721 Oak Street. Rough, unpainted concrete block formed the walls, and the floor, also concrete, spread out cracked and uneven. Dusty cobwebs draped the four ground-level windows. A discarded fuel oil tank hunkered in one corner. We used the room chiefly as a laundry and, occasionally, as a refuge from unending heat—the basement's temperature remained reliably cool even at the height of summer. On this July evening, however, we took refuge not from heat but from wind. We were grateful to be below ground.

The children had arranged one of their blankets on the hard floor and nestled among their most valued possessions: John clutched his collection of Matchbox cars; Katie, her photos of a trip taken with the grandparents; Christina, her stuffed animals and favorite picture books; and Andy, his foreign coin collection. Their pale faces bloomed in the semi-darkness as we descended the basement stairs. Katie gripped the dog, who looked uneasily at us and thumped her tail.

"Let's read a story!" I said cheerily, pulling at the chain of an overhead light bulb and thinking to myself that it had looked very green outside, green being the color I most often associated with tornadoes. We settled on the blanket, and I paged through the well-worn fairy tale book until I found an old favorite: "The Princess on the Glass Hill." *Once upon a time there was a man,* I began.

Through the tiny windows, I could tell that the sky had grown even darker. I could see a single dandelion, emerald blades of grass, the base of the spruce tree. It began to rain. Then it stopped. A strange silence seemed to enfold us. *So when evening came,* I read, *he set off to the barn* (What is happening outside? I wondered.) *and lay down to sleep.* (Why is it so quiet?) *But a little on in the night came such a clatter, and such an earthquake, that the walls and roof shook.* (Why has the wind died down? Could I hear the "freight train" roar of a tornado if it were near us?)

Then up jumped the lad and took to his heels as fast as ever he could. The ordinary house noises—the freezer's hum, the de-humidifier's rattle—claimed our ears. *Nor dared he once look round till he reached home.* We didn't have a clue about the intensity of the storm above us, which had already mowed through Cambridge, destruction and disruption in its wake. Abruptly, without fanfare, the electric light blinked once, then went out. With it went the hum of the appliances. The six of us sat in darkness and silence, the only light filtering in from the narrow slits of the basement windows. At eight o'clock, it looked like deepest night.

The story ended with the extinguished electricity, and we focused reluctantly on the storm. Our neighborhood often lost power when a certain vulnerable transformer was hit by lightning. Is that why the lights went out? Or had a tornado knocked out something else, perhaps at the power plant? Silence reigned. We waited—perhaps fifteen minutes, perhaps less: time gets distorted when destruction seems imminent—and listened. The minutes sauntered by as we sat in suspense. Some time later, we heard rain lash at the windows and then the grumble of a thunderstorm. The tension created by the silence and the suspension of the rain dissipated, and we relaxed a bit. Thunder and lightning were familiar; eerie quietude was not.

An hour later, the battery-run radio gave us an all-clear signal, and we climbed the stairs and put the children to bed. The remnants of the storm whipped North Branch late into the night, with sheets of rain and streaks of lightning.

The next morning dawned clear and sunny, and we assessed the damage. We learned that a twister had wound its way through town only two blocks from us, uprooting trees in Central Park, ruffling shingles off roofs, flipping an unoccupied camping trailer. Destruction appeared patchy, here and there: some houses untouched, others with damage. A tornado catches communities off guard. It drops from the heavens, stirs up trouble, and vanishes. This time, North Branch had been let off easy. On Oak Street, the wind had not even managed to knock my tiny green tomatoes off the vine.

In reading through thirty years of *North Branch Reviews* chronicling the town's early history, I noticed two great forces that periodically destroyed human endeavors. The first of these was fire; the second, tornadoes. Nearly every town in east-central Minnesota entertained a devastating fire (and, often, two or three) that destroyed wooden buildings in the downtown business district. And, despite their erratic behavior, tornadoes could be predicted as surely as the seasons. A summer without tornadoes was rare indeed.

North Branch knew both types of destruction. In 1892, what would become the first of several noteworthy fires engulfed a general store, the meat market, and a saloon. Two years later, some North Branchers witnessed firsthand the utter annihilation of Hinckley, thirty miles north on the railroad line. The worst fire in Minnesota history reduced Hinckley to ashes one dry fall day, with heat so intense that it melted the steel railroad tracks.

In 1914, North Branch hosted its own conflagration when a chimney fire in a second-floor photography gallery spread to engulf nine businesses and lay waste to the entire eastern end of Main Street. The fire, occurring shortly before Christmas, might have been quickly extinguished had the outdated fire equipment (purchased after the 1892 fire) functioned properly. Fifteen minutes into battle, the decrepit engine broke down, rendering the town helpless in the face of the blaze. The fire's glow could be seen twenty miles north at Pine City, its firemen joining others from Rush City to come to North Branch's aid. But without water, nothing could be done. This 1914 fire, which some in town still remember, is why North Branch looks so new—and plain—today. Many Main Street buildings, built of brick or concrete block, date from that fire. People wearied of watching frame structures burn.

Storms, too, took their toll. On June 6, 1906, at six o'clock in the evening, a tornado ripped through central Chisago County. First touching down in Wyoming, where it left houses and barns "twisted like kindling wood," it snaked its way north through tiny Stacy, reducing the town to matchsticks, then continued on toward North Branch. The tornado skirted town but splintered the county poor farm's barn, which stood two miles out. The farm's superintendent, Knute Blomgren, rode out the storm inside the massive house, his foot wedged against the front door to keep it in place. When terrific pressure forced the door open, his toe was shattered and eventually amputated, one of the noted casualties in a storm that killed only two people. The north branch of the Sunrise River also fell victim: eyewitnesses claimed that as the funnel passed over the creek it sucked out the water and carried it away.

Not many people alive today remember the 1906 storm, but those who do, residing now at Green Acres Nursing Home (built, coincidentally, on the former site of the poor farm), recall one salient feature: "It happened on the sixth day of the sixth month at six o'clock in '06—all those sixes!" they'll tell you, a meaningful glint in their eyes.

More people remember the horrendous storm of 1942, the one that killed Charlie Strait, the long-time owner of the town's livery stable. Although some folks refer to the event as a tornado, it may have been straight-line winds that swept into town around the supper hour on September 11. "Cyclonic winds," as the *Review* called them, created a path of destruction two to four miles wide, uprooting and snapping trees like twigs, obliterating buildings, and downing power and telephone lines. The storm destroyed the Farmers Produce Company warehouse and the Zeien Oil Company bulk plant as well. Despite the death and destruction accompanying the storm, the *Review's* account included the wry observation that a return of *Gone with the Wind* ("Coming soon!") was advertised on the marquee of the downtown Family Theater.

The townspeople mourned the dramatic loss of their beautiful trees. In the country, the destruction of forty barns stunned the populace. Because the storm struck during evening milking hours, many barns harbored dairy cows that became trapped inside when the barns blew down. The injured and dying animals had to be shot to end their suffering. Charlie Strait's fate was entwined with that of his animals.

Charlie Strait was seventy years old in 1942, a well-known and beloved citizen. He had come to town shortly after the turn of the century and soon assumed ownership of North Branch's livery. The town suited him and he settled down, marrying the post-master's daughter, Lulu Rowell, and raising a family. As the auto-mobile took hold in society, a livery became less and less needed. Charlie invested modestly, and ultimately unwisely, in the stock market and, like so many others, lost money in the 1929 crash. After this discouragement, he and Lu turned to dairy farming. He was in the barn milking his Jersey cows when the western sky blackened. As the wind hit, the barn flattened, reduced to tangled wreckage. Too late, Charlie sought refuge—the kindly man was found hours later, outside, under the barn door, which had blown outward. The injured cows, trapped in their stanchions, moaned in pain. A young neighbor, aiding in the rescue efforts, took his Colt revolver, crawled under the strewn rafters, and, one by one, put them down.

The lack of electricity and telephone service hindered rescue efforts and attempts to assess the full damage of the storm. People would clear trees, demolish stumps, clean up broken glass, and repair roofs for weeks and months. The storm itself would never leave them. Bellows of anguished animals echoed in their memories.

A few years after our North Branch storm, a massive tornado, half a mile wide, swept across southern Minnesota, destroying half of historic St. Peter as well as Gustavus Adolphus College, perched on the river bluff above town. A freakish, intensely violent storm, it went down in Minnesota history as one of only six tornadoes ever recorded in March. Glass exploded from windows. Elegant old buildings of yellow brick and kasota stone, Victorian houses with gingerbread trim, shattered as if bombs had blasted them. The college lost twenty thousand trees, St. Peter another twenty thousand. The tornado instantly denuded one of the state's oldest communities, wresting from the soil in five minutes' time arboreal shelter planted to counteract the vastness of the prairie sky.

The news of St. Peter's disaster hit our family like a blow to the solar plexus. Both graduates of Gustavus, Tom and I cherished memories of St. Peter and of the college going back to childhood. While many of the small towns in Minnesota boast only of utilitarian main streets, no-frills storefronts, and functional, white clapboard houses, St. Peter, because of its age, was different. Dignified, old-matron houses adorned with curlicue trim and gabled roofs, crafted from Minnesota's old-growth pine and maple when the state was young, were smashed as quickly as the rapidly built tract housing had been by the Cambridge storm. The tornado hadn't made distinctions.

The loss of the trees anguished the community. The college had been shaded by bur oaks, elms, sugar maples, and cedars. St. Peter's streets were lined with maples that flamed with oranges and yellows in the fall; tall cottonwoods towered over parks and neighborhoods. In a brief rush of wind, the prairie reclaimed its own.

Americans have conducted a love affair with nature that runs hot and cold. Poets write flowery verse, painters produce lavish canvases of romantic landscapes awash in golden tones, and theologians see the hand of God in the delicacy of a blossom or the finely wrought structure of a bird's wing. Conversely, we have at the same time been hog-tying wilderness into submission, paving it, tidying it up, bending it to our will.

But in the eerie green light of a tornado cloud, our love affair with nature, however tender or controlling, becomes meaningless. Our sense of devastation, helplessness, and loss in the wake of a destructive storm has not been alleviated by technology. Nature still presents to us a blank, unreadable face—omnipotent, omnipresent, and, most fearful of all, indifferent.

Do we love nature at the height of a storm? It is like asking, "Do we love God?" The scale of the would-be object of our affection is beyond human comprehension.

The reverse question, "Does nature love us?" seems absurd. Yet nature nurtures us in a fundamental way. We human beings have evolved to eat, seek shelter, and produce children under nature's bountiful rules. From the ticking of our hearts to the sighing of our lungs, we are immersed in a natural rhythm to which we must adhere.

I find it fitting that we head for the cellar when the wind begins to blow. To cower in the earth is a proper response to majesty.

Warmer

ON MIDSUMMER DAY, June 24, 1988, I awoke before dawn, before the summer's bird chorus began, and went upstairs to write. My desk edged a south-facing window, and from the second floor I looked out over my garden. I watched the solstice sun rise and illumine the skimpy rows of lettuce and beans clinging for dear life to the sandy soil. We were in the midst of a severe drought. It had not rained since Mother's Day, and as we entered June the days had turned exceptionally hot. My garden required daily watering, first to nudge seeds into sprouting, then to salvage tender seedlings. I drew water from a shallow sand-point well dug near the garden, then worried that the well would go dry.

We also used the well to fill the plastic wading pool that we maintained for our young children. The children, ages five, three, and one, suffered the common maladies of hot weather: heat rash, sunburn, lethargy, and sweaty irritability. We used the pool to alleviate some of these woes, spending the afternoons sprawled on lawn chairs and beach towels or splashing in the water and racing through the sprinkler.

We had already discovered that North Branch lawns went dormant with any rainless spell. The underlying sand could not retain moisture. The backyard grass had bleached straw-colored in late May and crunched under our bare feet. By June, it spread lifeless before us, a parched ecru shag carpet. Even the imperturbable bur oaks, watered by massive taproots, ran a water deficit on ninety-degree days. By four o'clock in the afternoon, their leaves hung limp and dark, victims of over-transpiration, not to be restored to vigor until the cool of night. I had the sense during these searing afternoons that we were living not in Minnesota but someplace far away, perhaps in Wyoming or eastern Montana, someplace west, where water is scarce and life is marked by aridity.

Writing at my desk on Midsummer morning after a string of ninety-degree days, I recorded how we were coping with the heat and the drought and our sense of growing despair as each evening we scanned the western horizon in vain for rain clouds.

At six, I heard the thud of the newspaper landing on the front steps and went downstairs to claim it. The oaken front door hung open to invite in the cool sigh of early morning. The *Minneapolis Star Tribune* lay covering a litter of tiny green acorns that had dropped from the front yard trees. As I bent down to pick up the paper, I read the bold print headlines: "Warm Up of Earth Has Begun, Congress Warned." Beneath was a photo of NASA scientist James Hansen testifying before a congressional hearing that he believed we were experiencing the first symptoms of an enhanced greenhouse effect.

Time seemed to arrest in that moment. I became acutely aware of the rustle of oak leaves, the prick of tiny acorns on my feet, the blue of the seersucker robe wrapped around my body. When I read that headline, I think my heart stopped beating. Surely it must have, because when it resumed and I came back to life, I entered a new world.

· · · ·

The "greenhouse effect" is what the *Star Tribune* called it in 1988, when the phenomenon made headline news for the first time. Today we use the term "global warming," which more accurately describes what is happening to the earth's climate. A very small amount of carbon dioxide, measured in parts per million, has an immense capacity to retain the sun's heat in our atmosphere. We know that for a fact. It is also a fact that the amount of carbon dioxide in the atmosphere is 30 percent higher than it was in pre-industrial times. Another fact: the eleven warmest years since the invention of the thermometer occurred in the eighties and nineties. The warmest year in the thousand-year reconstruction of past temperatures over the northern hemisphere: 1998.

We peer into the near future and use computers to gauge the rise in temperature caused by increasing levels of carbon dioxide. Models predict that, on average, the earth will warm by as much as seven degrees Fahrenheit. In Minnesota, however, the change in our average annual temperatures will be more extreme. Because our state is situated in the middle of a continent, temperature rise will not be moderated by the oceans. Fort Snelling records dating from 1860, the oldest records in the state, show an increase of 2.9 degrees already, whereas overall the average global land temperature has risen only half that—about 1.5 degrees.

We think of Minnesota as a forested state, but in actuality the region has been caught in a perpetual tug-of-war between the western edge of the great deciduous forest to the east and the Great Plains to the west. The presence of savanna attests to the divide. In the last ten thousand years, prairie has advanced eastward during periods of extended dryness while trees have marched westward during wet cycles.

It is hard for computer models to predict exactly how far into the center of a warmer continent the air masses that bring sufficient amounts of rainfall will intrude. If rainfall decreases, as some models show, we can expect Minnesota to become like present-day Nebraska. If we receive enough rainfall to support trees, the state might look like Ohio. But this would not happen immediately. After all, our current trees—conifers like pines and spruce and broadleaves like maples and basswood—are adapted to the past centuries' cool climate. Foresters expect to see forest dieback soon in Minnesota, perhaps by 2010. Thus, although we might have a type of mature forest in parts of Minnesota in two hundred years, during the interim—when we and our children and our grandchildren will live out our lives—we will view a landscape of dead snags, scrubby brush, and (hopefully) small, warm-adapted seedlings.

That is the rosier of the two scenarios. If Minnesota receives less rainfall than it does now, our forests could become savannas, especially where the underlying soil is sandy. Researchers have created computer models for northern Minnesota based on soil type. In our beloved Boundary Waters, the towering pines that presently grow on sandy soils will not be able to take the heat of a 3.6-degree temperature rise. Models predict oak savanna, brushy scrub, and grassland will replace them. Time span to reach a 3.6-degree rise: fifty years.

Unlike most Minnesotans who read their morning *Tribune* on June 24, 1988, I knew about the greenhouse effect, having been introduced to the idea in my college ecology course fifteen years earlier. A description took up one paragraph in our textbook. Scientists had feared for decades that the release of carbon dioxide in the combustion of fossil fuels would one day be large enough to affect the climate. But, back in 1971, when Eugene Odum's *Fundamentals of Ecology* was published, the time span in which this would occur was thought to be four hundred years. Earth had recently experienced a cooling trend, and our class hadn't dwelt on the opposite possibility.

Nevertheless, it had always been there in the back of my mind, the fear of the greenhouse effect. A few years earlier, we'd had one warm, dry winter with almost no snow—uncommon, but not unheard of. It was followed by a hot, dry summer the year my third baby was born. The summer drought of 1988 came the next year. I think I was always worrying subconsciously.

. . . .

History sheds some light on what may be in store for the Anoka Sand Plain and the North Branch area. During the prolonged drought of the 1930s, certain sandy areas couldn't support any vegetation. Blow-out areas, where prevailing winds scoured the earth's surface bare and left bowl-like indentations, can be seen today at the Helen Allison Savanna. Shifting sand dunes reappeared after being protected by prairie grasses for thousands of years, and they remain devoid of plant cover even now, after decades of "normal" rainfall.

Today, very few native plants grow on the Anoka Sand Plain. At present, we gaze out on suburban lawns and agricultural fields—prime candidates for wind erosion in a drier climate (think dust bowl). The lawns are primarily bluegrass, which is not adapted for drier conditions and needs to be maintained by irrigation. Imagine all the residents drawing water from the underlying aquifer to sprinkle their lawns. Imagine how quickly that aquifer will draw down when we no longer have abundant rain to replenish it. Imagine a dry, dry world, where grass crinkles underfoot.

A dropping water table has other implications. Throughout the Anoka Sand Plain, the water table is uneven, sometimes rising very near the surface. An aerial view reveals a generous sprinkling of lakes and cattail marshes across the sand plain counties, areas that today remain undeveloped and harbor a wealth of wildlife. But computer scenarios for small marshes like these are not favorable. Forecasts for the prairie pothole region of western Minnesota suggest that we will lose half of these wetlands by 2050. The homes of waterfowl and other wildlife will evaporate.

Perhaps I glimpsed the future when I returned to the Helen Allison Savanna this spring. We had enjoyed a rainy April, but it followed on the heels of two dry years. The swale, where on Mother's Day ten years ago we had discovered seven species of frogs, was dry. And, of course, devoid of amphibians.

At first I thought I could beat the rap of climate change, that I, personally, could turn this thing around. I thought of all the ways our family put carbon dioxide into the atmosphere, and we began to cut back. In retrospect, my efforts remind me of a cancer victim trying to fight the disease with herbal tea and positive thinking.

North Branch is a great walk-about town, and we intensified our efforts to get by without a car. The children began walking to school, a distance of five blocks. The school district ran buses through the neighborhood, but our kids "set a good example." I began bicycling to the grocery store whenever possible, using the child trailer—often filled with two sacks and two small children—to haul groceries home. We set our thermostat at sixty-five degrees. We bought an insulative jacket for the hot water heater, and we didn't buy an air conditioner.

We bought a compact car that got fifty miles to a gallon of gasoline, the best technology on the market. When our second car broke down and needed replacement, I held out for a month (during which we hauled six people around in the compact), insisting we didn't need a grand van, or air conditioning, or automatic transmission. After weeks of searching, our dealer located in Two Harbors a "small" mini-van that had a stick shift—one of two in the state. But it had air conditioning. That "option" is standard on minivans: if we wanted one without AC, we needed to special order from Detroit and pay two thousand dollars to not have it installed.

Since cows produce methane, and methane is a potent greenhouse gas, we cut back on eating beef. I planned one vegetarian meal per week and introduced the family to black beans, lentil spaghetti sauce, chickpea hummus, and buckaroo pinto beans. We started producing our own methane supply on that diet, and the kids missed their hamburgers. But they were young: I figured they'd adapt.

Most significant for me was a return to teaching. An inquiry at the local community college landed a gem of an assignment: Environmental Science. The course was a mix of natural science, ecology, and environmental issues. I began the quarter lecturing on food chains, nutrient cycling, and population dynamics. Then, using the ecological concepts already developed, we moved into the knotty environmental problems: overpopulation, ozone depletion, extinction, and, of course, global warming. Three years had passed since NASA scientist James Hansen testified before Congress, and now educational materials abounded. Public television shows like the *Race to Save the Planet* series snagged the interest of my visually oriented young students. Common wisdom in the early 1990s said we had ten years in which to begin addressing the issue of global warming. The clock was ticking.

After five years of teaching Environmental Science quarter after quarter, five years of listening to an earnest Meryl Streep, host of *Race to Save the Planet*, tell us, "We're all in this together," my zeal wore out. I still believed that global warming was the greatest threat our living planet had ever faced, but my ears heard my teaching voice and it sounded strident. Was I too much the advocate and not enough the dispassionate scholar? Was I slanting the course? Had I crossed the line from teaching to preaching? Small whispers of doubt buzzed in my ear. When they grew loud enough, I quit. I had a life to live. My personal race to save the planet was over.

The life I live is marked by the seasons, the presence and absence of rain and snow, the coming and leaving of birds. When I entered the world at birth, myrtle warblers foraged in the elms lining Park Avenue in south Minneapolis; when I left the hospital with my parents one week later, Tennessee warblers sang from bur oak treetops and feasted on catkins. I know this because the rhythms of migrating warblers are predictable, timed to coincide with the blooming of the trees. The strange, prehistoric loon's song marked summer days at the lake. The first thin swirls of snow flurries brought slate-colored juncos to our backyard feeder. Six weeks later, the saying went, look for permanent snow.

My days are more than a mere progression of square white boxes on a calendar page. They are suffused with the scent of the earth—the cold smell of snow, the sweet odor of wet soil, the fragrance of wild plum. Not only my body but also my imagination lives in the natural world. I look for February shadows on snow, their shapes telling me the equinox is approaching. The cherry-colored flowers of the red maple, those first blooms of spring, cheer me even when snow remains at the end of a long winter. In my mind, I recount the thousands of winters my ancestors have endured in a northern climate, witnessing the stark beauty of a January night, its snow and stars and frigid air. Winter is my birthright, a birthright I thought I would bequeath to my descendants.

Long ago, in the same year I took the ecology course, I was enrolled in Christian Ethics. In class, we discussed values and guiding principles and the fast pace of technological change. My professor, a visionary, was excited by futuristic projections. In an assignment, he asked us to envision our lives in the year 2000: How will we work? Play? Raise families? Where will we live? What will we believe in?

A biology major, I chose my field because I had come to believe that human beings were fundamentally animals and that an understanding of biology would explain much of why humans act as they do. Before people were psychological beings, or spiritual beings, or language users, or artists, they were biological beings, and understanding this earthy base was the first step, I thought, in understanding the world.

When I tried to imagine my life in 2000, I thought not of robots doing my housework, nor of pills providing a full plate of nutrition. Instead, I conjured up a family—husband and children—work as a teacher, a quiet life. I thought there might be war. As a college student in 1973, I was acutely conscious of the evil of war, but I thought it was useless to anticipate what form social upheaval, whether from war or from other symptoms of overpopulation, might take. I thought I could counteract the swirl of social change by cultivating friendships, a love of books and music, a nurturing family life— all of which had been a comfort and an inspiration for people over the millennia. I would remember to take pleasure in physical exertion, pleasure in my animal body. And, above all, I would keep close to nature—aware of the moons and stars shifting in the heavens, aware of the great wheel of seasons that brings us snow in December and rain in April, delight in the intricacy of birds. I promised myself to be mindful.

Suddenly, more quickly than I believed possible, it is 2000, and I am living my future. I am married and have children and revel in the stimulation of books and music. No robot does my housework (alas) and no pill provides my complete diet (thank goodness). I am surrounded by a wealth of friends. In fact, I have everything I ever imagined, except the one thing of which I was most sure: the constancy of nature.

While my social and intellectual lives are awash in blessings, my animal self, that most basic, earthy self, wonders if it will have a home, if its brothers and sisters in earth's ecosystems will survive the coming century. Now when snowflakes fall on a cold November night, there is a catch in my throat. I hear migrating loons at dawn in May and feel the presence of these northern birds is a miracle. Nature's constancy, promised in Genesis, of "seedtime and harvest, cold and heat, summer and winter" is no longer a given.

Can we turn down the heat? Might we, by our actions, make good the Genesis promise? Even in the darkest night, ancient sailors had stars to navigate by. Here are some stars: in Minnesota, even non-environmentalists are talking more about developing wind power and less about drilling for more oil; Honda and Toyota offer cars with hybrid engines that get over fifty miles to the gallon, and hybrid SUVs are on the horizon; British Petroleum brags in *Newsweek* ads that it is one of the world's largest producers of solar panels.

After fifty years of relentless oppression, the Berlin Wall came down overnight. Overnight—without warning or fanfare. The many small changes that toppled the wall had been hidden from the public eye.

The clock is still ticking. The hour has not yet struck. It is possible that one day we, too, might wake and find that the world has changed.

The King of North Branch

THE TRIM, DAPPER MAN leans in toward the wide-eyed clinic receptionist. His face is smooth-shaven, he wears a tie, and no one would ever call him elderly, though, at ninety years, that's what he is. His voice twangs with vigor. "What do you mean, you don't know who I am? Why, I'm the king of North Branch!"

Indeed, I think to myself, raising my eyebrows as my husband relates this story to me. Well, it wouldn't be the first time a king was self-anointed.

I don't really know what to think of Clayton Anderson. In our little kingdom of North Branch, Clayton Anderson has ruled for decades. If you believe his version of history, the scepter has been handed down through generations, as his family built the railroad, grew the first potatoes, and constructed the Lutheran church and most of the village's houses. (There is some truth in all these claims.) Among the townspeople he is by turns revered, disliked, and feared. Charming by first inclination, he has cajoled, bullied, and manipulated North Branchers throughout his seventy years of civic life. Though his political and economic machinations have always benefited his own concerns, they have also usually served the wider community good as well.

Clayton has personally experienced ninety of the town's 130 years of existence, and even now his memory is sharp. I love to listen to his stories because he is crisp and authoritative in his interpretation of North Branch history. But Clayton doesn't live in the past. That is clearly evident as I stand at his front door one morning, prepared to interview him. Beyond the door, in his office off the kitchen, he is at work at his desk. Because he suffers from macular degeneration, he is aided by a large, brightly lit magnifying glass, which he bends over, studying receipts. Messy stacks of papers, documents, news clippings, and envelopes tower over his work space. Watching him, I suspect that he keeps his fingers in so many pies that even in great age his endeavors still consume him.

At the sound of my knock, he stumps to the door to greet me, cane in hand. He is dressed in a wool plaid shirt, a dark tie neatly knotted at his neck. With feisty good cheer, he waves a letter from the county auditor containing the Chisago County year 2000 census data. The numbers, he assures me, will make it possible for North Branch to capture the county seat.

I stifle a small smile as I follow him into the sunny breakfast room where we will talk. North Branch's attempts to wrest the county seat from Center City are legendary. The war has been waged for over a hundred years. Since the building of the railroad in 1870, North Branch has been bigger, better situated on the lines of commerce, and more centrally located than tiny Center City, which even today numbers only 582 people. But, alas, Center City was older and full of promise when these things were decided in Minnesota. North Branch has chafed for decades.

As we settle ourselves at the glass-topped table, Clayton reminds me of the skullduggery surrounding the 1899 bid for the county seat. The treachery of the Rush City businessmen; the unwarranted loss of the county fairgrounds—politics, all politics! The kingdom was double-crossed! He conveniently ignores the most recent courthouse bid, conducted in 1994. Although Clayton had offered to donate land on which to build a new courthouse, the county voted decisively to retain Center City as the county seat. A gleaming white brick county government center was built on the shores of North Center Lake following the vote, and the issue seemed settled, at least for my lifetime. But apparently not for the king.

It's time to change the subject. I want to ask him today about the more recent past—about his years as a North Branch businessman (owner of the Ford dealership), about his land acquisition as the freeway came through. I want to hear about the map he drew up and affixed to a window shade, using it as a visual aid when he spoke to local civic groups. His plans for a new, prosperous North Branch included the courthouse (of course), a hospital, an airport, and a plethora of businesses. I'm hoping, not unreasonably, that the map is still around, buried in the morass of civic documents in his basement.

But before I can get my words out, Clayton is off and running on a slightly different tack. "You know all those new stores in Cambridge?" he asks, nodding his head west toward our neighboring town. He's referring to the "big-box" super stores that have invaded Cambridge in the last three years—the WalMart, the Menard's, the Target—with their acres and acres of paved parking lots, once soybean fields. "We could have had 'em here! Here in North Branch! They could have been ours [cane waving], if we'd had the courthouse!"

I set my own agenda aside. This is what I came to learn, anyway: Clayton's dreams for North Branch. For kings not only rule, they also envision a future. And though North Branch hasn't been graced with a WalMart or a Menard's, much of Clayton's vision has come to pass.

Life changed for America after World War II, and even small communities like North Branch were propelled into the future.

Franklin Roosevelt had proposed a system of "limited access" highways, modeled after the German autobahn, to link major U.S. cities. After the bombing of Hiroshima ushered in the atomic age, planners envisioned this freeway system as an evacuation route in the event of a nuclear attack. Congress provided heft to Roosevelt's proposal in 1956 when it committed the federal government to pay 90 percent of the construction costs.

Minnesota's share was a planned 914 miles of roadway. The initial phase produced a concrete ribbon that cut through the heart of the state's two major cities, obliterating urban neighborhoods and dislocating their people. When this construction was complete, the highway engineers turned their attention northward, with plans to link the Twin Cities to Minnesota's third-largest city and only international port, Duluth. The new road would traverse Chisago County, brushing North Branch's western edge.

The Twin Cities and Duluth had been linked three times before. In territorial times, a rough government road was hacked out of the wilderness. Then, in early statehood, entrepreneurs had funded construction of a railroad, completed in 1870, the project that had given birth to North Branch. Later, in the 1920s, helped by the 1916 Federal Aid Road Act, the state had constructed U.S. Highway 61 to accommodate the newly popular automobile. Each new artery had pumped lifeblood into the village. Local businesses and farmers relied on the Twin Cities markets; the town's citizens enjoyed easy access to city stores and entertainment. Situated on these two lines, North Branch flourished. This new fourth route—the freeway—would allow the town to keep pace with the post-war age.

The *North Branch Review* announced construction plans for the freeway in 1958. Later that year, the state highway department presented a tentative route to the North Branch Civic Club, promising citizen input at a future public hearing

Six months later, at the public hearing in the school's auditorium, it was clear how intrusive this freeway would be. Its heavy track on the landscape would indelibly affect many people's way of life. Although several county commissioners pronounced it a "good thing for Chisago County"—"We need these freeways," remarked one—the Farmers Union roared its opposition. One farmer compared the road to the Great Wall of China because it would bisect numerous farms. Farmers would have fields on both sides of the freeway—but no easy access to them, since roads over the freeway would be few in number. Some farmers anticipated traveling many miles on a slow-paced combine or dragging a plow simply to move from one field to another. The highway official replied that his department was well aware of the social problems created when a freeway crosses a community.

No additional public hearings would be held. Townships affected by the route would have no further opportunity to comment on the project. Only villages penetrated by the new road were allowed to approve or disapprove the final route. In Chisago County, the town of Stacy alone had this status.

The freeway would invade a pastoral world. In 1959, the North Branch community was still dependent on dairy farming, as it had been for several decades. Pretty girls with lovely smiles competed for the title "Princess Kay of the Milky Way," a dairy industry promotion. Firms offering artificial insemination of milk cows inserted ads on the back pages of the *Review*.

Like the rest of the nation, North Branchers grappled with the specter of nuclear holocaust. The American Legion Auxiliary held informational meetings on "How to Survive a Nuclear Attack" and provided plans for bomb shelters and instructions on how to lessen radiation exposure. North Branch considered peaceful uses of the atom, too. Fifty miles away, the first nuclear power reactor in the rural United States was under construction in Elk River, and many anticipated its cheap electricity.

The Space Age had dawned. At Thanksgiving, the Village Bakery advertised "Sputnik Pumpkin Pie," a delicacy that was really "out of this world." The Three Stooges starred in *Have Rocket, Will Travel* at the Family Theater. And Merchants State Bank featured an ad in which a young boy playing with a toy missile would "rocket into the future" with a banking account to assure his financial security. Children lined up for the new Salk vaccine against polio, and Minnesotans everywhere pondered a new concept called "daylight-saving time." Urban dwellers—of which there was an increasing number—by and large liked an additional hour of light at the end of the day. Farmers, on the other hand, were generally opposed and considered it confusing and unnatural to abandon "sun" time.

North Branch was changing. The Northern Pacific Railroad, a fixture so integral to town life as to be considered immutable, drastically reduced passenger service on its St. Paul to Duluth line because ridership had dwindled to "almost nothing." The U.S. Postal Service, which had used the railroad to transport mail since 1870, switched to trucks. Two natural gas pipelines were laid through the area, offering an alternative to fuel oil or coal, home heating fuels that had been the only option since the savanna's wood was exhausted around the turn of the century.

To cope with these changes, and anticipating the future construction of the freeway, the village council established a planning commission. Its first act was to hire a Minneapolis consulting firm to survey the town's facilities, analyze land use, and draw up a plan for future development so the village could manage its growth. When completed, the consulting firm's report in turn revealed even more changes. North Branch had gained more people in the decade from 1950–59 than it had in the forty previous years, growing more rapidly than the state as a whole. Less than half of the population had lived in North Branch for ten years. More than half worked outside of town. Some even worked as far away as the Twin Cities.

In 1959, Clayton Anderson, a brisk, efficient man in his prime, turned forty-nine. Decades before computers, fax machines, and cell phones, Clayton had already adopted multi-tasking as a way of life. A visit to the Ford show room in town might find him simultaneously pointing out the finer points of a Fairlane to an interested buyer, directing a mechanic on the proper way to tune an engine, and carrying on a furious phone conversation, receiver (cord attached) affixed to one ear. Jabbing at the air with an unlit cigar, he'd turn and greet you—a possible Ford owner, who knows?—with a vigorous "Hi! What can we do for you?"

Then there was his community involvement. In 1957, he spearheaded an ambitious but ultimately unsuccessful attempt to construct a municipal swimming pool for area residents. In 1958, he was one of eight men appointed to the new planning commission. In 1959, he introduced to North Branchers "a wonderful New World of Fords for 1960," including the immensely popular Thunderbird.

Then, in 1960, he began to buy land west of town.

Perhaps no one truly foresaw the changes the freeway would bring to North Branch. No one fully understood the implications of facilitated motor travel. People were not entirely heedless of the freeway's possibilities, of course. When they knew that I-35 would cross Chisago County, the commissioners embarked on the lengthy process of drawing up zoning and building regulations. And after the freeway's route was announced, the North Branch Civic Club quickly urged that the village begin comprehensive planning. But no one envisioned the sandy, marginal farmlands on the outskirts of town, the land the freeway would bisect, as suddenly, unimaginably valuable, except, perhaps, the King. Only Clayton knew that acreage had become real estate. Is this the point at which he truly took on the crown?

Chisago County's Section 20, just west of North Branch, a square of the Anoka Sand Plain, assumed a future that did not include soybeans and field corn. And, gradually, that section became Clayton Anderson's. Long before the road graders scraped the fine-grained soil, before the bulldozers and monstrous earth-moving caterpillars rumbled into town, Clayton added to his holdings until, in the end, he owned most of the land, including the corners of the interchange with Highway 95.

· · · · ·

By 1969, the freeway through Chisago County, the last link of Interstate 35 from the Twin Cities to Duluth, was completed. That decade, North Branchers had taken on new concerns and left others behind. No longer obsessed with surviving a nuclear war, people now worried about a new type of conflict in Vietnam. The *Review* reported regularly on the whereabouts of local servicemen and headlined, sadly, the first area man to be killed in action, a farm-boy-turned–Green Beret from Harris. Anti-war protests struck a nerve with townspeople. The *Review's* editor, Charles Meyer, ran as front-page news an opinion piece taken from *Minnesota Sheriff* magazine decrying civil disobedience as "the road to [the] loss of all liberties."

The environmental movement was taking root. A large tract of pristine land along the St. Croix River was being considered for protection as a wild waterway. Clayton's son, state senator Jerry Anderson, would soon sponsor legislation for a new local state park: Wild River.

Interstate 35 opened in November 1969 with great fanfare. Ceremonies were held at every bridge and overpass. Minnesota governor Harold Levander was on hand at the overpass in North Branch. The town's one thousand schoolchildren walked out to the freeway in the new-fallen snow to witness the event and cheer this tangible sign of progress. Wielding a pair of oversized scissors furnished by the North Branch Women's Civic Club, the Midsummer queen cut the ribbon, opening the new road. Lauded as part of "the largest public works in the history of men," I-35 was hailed as a bright, new beginning. "Its impact," the governor noted in a letter to the elementary school principal, "will be felt for many years to come."

How prescient was Governor Levander! In the decades that followed, the new freeway changed the face of North Branch forever.

Before freeway construction began, the village council asked the state highway department to shift the proposed route six hundred yards west to allow the downtown business district room to expand in its present location. This reasonable request, first proposed by North Branch's planning commission and later supported by the Chisago County commissioners, was denied. The same week that a city delegation met with the highway department, Clayton secured his first parcel of Section 20.

With North Branch hemmed in by the new road, the King began to build. His Ford dealership moved to the west side of the freeway, blanketing the former potato fields with parking lots. A bank went up west of the sprawling dealership. Later appeared a strip mall, then a second one, acres of asphalt laid down on the sand. A gas station popped up on the northeast corner of the interchange, a fast-food burger place to the southeast.

People couldn't walk to these businesses—nor were they meant to. Designed in the suburban mentality, they catered to the automobile. The scale fit cars, not people and horse-drawn wagons as the original downtown had. One might drive past a window and order a Happy Meal, but one couldn't enjoy a stroll through this section of town—there wasn't anything to stroll through, just a patchwork of parking lots and turn lanes and narrow boulevard strips with transplanted shrubbery.

Some possibilities lie outside even a king's realm. North Branch wasn't given the county government center or the new hospital: greater forces than Clayton Anderson's stubborn will controlled those destinies. But that which the King could ordain—freeway-oriented business, a full section of disorganized sprawl—came into being.

But did Clayton really have that much power? Perhaps *most* possibilities lie outside a king's realm. Once the federal government decreed that a freeway would cut through Chisago County, could the new road have been integrated into North Branch's pleasant village life in any other way?

In the 1950s, people had not had much time to think through freeway development. Limited-access highways were entirely new, and it would be years before people began decrying the ugliness and community disintegration that borders them. If there is an enduring truth about North Branch, it is that the community is a microcosm of greater American society. It is a mini-world. How could anyone suppose that North Branch's small section of freeway would escape the nation's fate?

Today's North Branch community lives with that fate. The businesses designed solely for cars attract cars. Automobiles pass back and forth over the freeway bridge in alarming numbers. A bridge designed to accommodate a community entirely on one side of the freeway now carries heavy traffic moving in both directions. At certain times of the day, the congestion backs up half a mile, and emergency vehicles dispatched from their downtown stations sit stalled with the masses. The smell of exhaust hangs on the air.

Parked to one side of the Anderson driveway is an old blue and white pickup, a Ford, of course. Battered and rusted, it looks like it has bounced down a fair number of back roads in its lifetime. After our first conversation a year ago, Clayton had wanted to escort me in his truck, had wanted to show me something. But, recalling the magnifying lens, the cane, and the fact that his sons didn't want him to drive, I had responded with an uneasy smile, a murmured regret, and a quick dash to my own car.

However, Clayton is nothing if not tenacious. On each subsequent visit, he invited me for a ride in that truck. I parried as well as I could. Finally, on this clear blue September day, I have decided to risk it. It is two days after the World Trade Center terrorist attacks, and all of life seems dicey. I am somehow destined for that truck. Clayton offers to let me drive while he rides in the passenger seat. "Now don't misunderstand," he assures me. "You'll do the driving and only on my property."

I climb into the cab, noting the gaping holes in the floorboard, the green grass below. I wonder how old the truck is. The engine rumbles like a big cat, then dampens to a purr as I shift into "drive" and head out. We bobble east on ruts through a soybean field, headed for North Branch Creek, the term North Branchers have always used for this section of the Sunrise River. The pretty, little river winds through the far border of the Anderson property.

Perhaps it's been awhile since Clayton has ridden in his beloved truck, I think sentimentally, as soybeans fly by, visible through the hole beneath my feet. Perhaps it's a genuine pleasure for him to get a chance to survey his land. (I learn later that my noble feelings of "helping" are misplaced: he drives frequently and defiantly.) The air is cool, insects buzz, and the sun is warm and yellow at midday. Suddenly I consider the efficacy of the brakes—a nice thing to have as we roll down to the river. High-strung by nature, I briefly envision the hood nosed into the creek, Clayton and me trapped in the cab, water swirling up through the holes in the floor. Death by drowning.

The brakes work. "Turn here," Clayton instructs. We leave the bean field and pass under a sign proclaiming "Little Sweden." I take a small, sharp breath at the scene before us.

A serene greenish light invades the shadows of this September day. Summer's verdure is still intact but fading. Below us flows the serpentine Sunrise, a single yellow maple leaf floating starlike on its surface. Burly oaks and wispy soft maples grow along the banks. The Andersons have left the river and its banks mostly untouched, though a footpath winds along the water's edge. I can see a fire pit lined with big stones in one spot, a picnic table and a trash can complete with a liner nearby. I imagine a younger Clayton roasting hot dogs with his boys or with his grandchildren—with even his great-grandchildren. It is a place to play, to build a fire and sit around it, to watch the river flow. I stare off into the distance, trying to conjure up the hard-bitten, fast-talking Clayton in old clothes, picnicking.

Clayton urges me to get out, to have a look around, something he can no longer do. He himself is out the door, prodding the sandy, grassy earth with his cane, looking expectant, as if he has handed me a present.

In sandals and a knit dress, I cautiously pick my way to the river. Poison ivy, large and lush, dots the edges of the path. Sunlight dapples the river's water, which is crystalline to its sandy bottom. Overhead, an old bur oak with dusty leaves blocks the brightness of the sky. Small, green fall warblers flit within its boughs. The loveliness of the scene is arresting precisely because it is what I least expected. Clayton boasting—yes. Clayton flexing muscle—yes. But Clayton harboring the sweet heart of the Sunrise River? Never.

"Follow the path! It goes on," he tells me from above. "I'll meet you where it comes out."

I hear the truck door slam and the engine start up. "Oh, God, no, he's driving," I think. Dismayed and—I have to admit it—amused, I wonder if he actually is a threat to himself. Or to the truck. Or to me.

The path passes through a thick understory of hazel bushes, their tiny birchlike "cones" perfectly formed. I thread through it, thinking how nice it must have been for the Andersons to have this wild space, tucked away within the town itself, as a retreat. When I come to an outer loop in the path, Clayton is waiting for me "You're a good sport," he tells me, not realizing how thrilled I am to see a portion of the river I'd never seen before. When I ask him if I can come back to watch birds, he says, "of course."

He shows no sign of relinquishing the wheel, and I am at a loss for how to regain the driver's seat. So I climb into the passenger's side and fasten my seat belt, thinking, "How did this happen, Sue? How did this happen?" and praying for a safe ten minutes.

As Clayton heads the truck west, up the field to the house, I wonder how much he can see. He must be able to see the ruts in the field. Could he see a dog straying in his path? A hole? As we jostle along, he mentions he'll be extra careful because we can't have the Doctor's Wife getting in an accident.

Clayton the Farmer stops to inspect the soybeans, which are not as mature as he would like. They need three more weeks of warm weather to produce a good yield.

Clayton the Philanthropist points out his immense pumpkin patch, out of which will come round, orange pumpkins for all the town's elementary-school children. "You gotta be careful," he remarks. "You gotta have enough. Because if even *one child* doesn't get a pumpkin—that's no good." Philanthropy is in the details.

Clayton the Gardener parks the truck and leads me to his plot, ripe with red tomatoes and glossy eggplants. I leave with melons, peppers, eggplants, and a five-gallon pail of tomatoes. "Come back for more," he tells me. "Come back any time."

I find as I drive off down the street that I am not thinking about kings anymore. How easy and satisfying it would be to see Clayton Anderson as the villain, with his bullying ways and his unreflective embrace of Progress. It is, after all, the unsophisticated assumption that bigger is better—bigger roads, bigger stores, bigger houses, bigger communities—that has led us into the snarled knot of backed-up traffic, strip malls, acres of asphalt, and empty downtown storefronts. Why is it that people like things big?

Yet Clayton is more than a man simply and fatally attracted to progress. The bite of his intellect attracts me—his proclivity to apply his business acumen to the local scene, his interest in carving a significant future role for North Branch, his ability to secure a place for himself in history. It intrigues me that this thrust toward power and control exists side by side with a nature that is protective of a pristine creek, generous to schoolchildren, and pleased when round, red tomatoes ripen in the garden. Clayton's interest in nurturing the small and particular might once have turned North Branch into something much different and more to my liking. Instead, North Branch has become merely big—and bland.

To be truly at home in the future, we need visions as complex as we are.

Growing Houses

WHEN I WAS A FIFTH GRADER at Lake Owasso Elementary School in Roseville, Minnesota, my classroom overlooked a cornfield that skirted a marsh on the south side of the lake. In quiet moments, when I probably should have been reading, I'd watch the farmer at work—picking corn, piling pumpkins onto a hayrack, and, later, turning the earth under, preparing the field for winter. But that field was never returned to corn or alfalfa. Instead, the following spring it grew the final crop: houses, suburban-style ramblers that sprang up to join the neighborhood already at its edge.

The disappearance of that field was just one of many losses I witnessed during my growing-up years. The magnificent sliding hill west of the school was cut and terraced for an apartment complex. That same project filled in the marsh we used as a skating pond. Across the railroad tracks, a larger part of the marsh was dredged to become a bona fide lake, the centerpiece for Roseville's

Central Park. The field north of our house, which had harbored pheasants and meadowlarks, large gardens and a horse pasture, was bisected by a road. Twenty houses followed. Another field became a nursing home with an extensive parking lot that drained off to Lake Owasso. Marshes, oak woods, "vacant lots"—places where small, wild animals might live—all went to houses during my eighteen years in Roseville.

My hometown was originally settled as a farming community and for nearly a century fed the Twin Cities from its truck gardens and dairies. Remnants of this past can still be seen in the greenhouses lining Larpenteur Avenue, and the plots of land behind them. When my parents bought a small lot from a Roseville farmer in 1955, they were participating in the first great burgeoning of urban expansion following World War II.

In retrospect, Roseville "filled" with astonishing speed. As a girl, I did not know that what was happening to Roseville had a name, or that it was a widespread occurrence. I only knew that the loss of the fields, of the woods and marshes, of the small spaces of wildness, was painful. It was a process I never wanted to live through again.

When Tom and I moved to North Branch in 1984, we were attracted to its small-town qualities. We wanted to live in town so we could walk to stores, and we found a house two doors west of the medical clinic. Tom could walk to work.

A family doctor, Tom had trained for a rural practice. Family practitioners out in the country generally enjoy a more varied and challenging practice than those in clinics where there are many specialists. Country docs routinely deliver babies, set bones, and work in emergency rooms. Some even do C-sections. "It's the best of both worlds," Tom's soon-to-be colleagues assured us. "Family practice is strong here, and yet, if you want to go into the Cities for a concert or the Guthrie, it's only a forty-five-minute drive."

It was true. Tom's practice quickly grew busy; I found a part-time teaching job at the local community college, and, like Mr. and

Mrs. Mallard in Robert McCloskey's book, we found it to be "just the right place to hatch ducklings."

Sometime during our second decade in town, this small-town appeal began to change. One morning after returning from patient rounds at the hospital in Chisago City, Tom walked into the kitchen, slid his backpack on the table, and said, "You know, sooner or later, Audubon is going to have to address the problem of zoning. There are houses going up all over the place."

I was disconcerted to hear Tom talk about zoning. The term seemed relegated to civic matters, something of only marginal interest to me. But now that he'd said the word, I realized that each month seemed to bring a new house or two, springing up unexpectedly, like mushrooms after a rain. Farms that we thought were fully functional would suddenly sprout little pink-flagged stakes. A sandy, proto-driveway would appear in the middle of a soybean field, followed quickly by a concrete block foundation, then a frame. Soon there'd be a house where there hadn't been one before. I began to feel echoes of Roseville.

Our Wild River Audubon chapter wasn't keen to take on the issue of zoning. Plat maps, building codes—it seemed like pretty dry stuff. Public policy involving land use had never been one of our discussion topics. We enjoyed watching birds together in the spring and canoeing the Sunrise River. But one day, Chisago County's state senator—a fellow Auduboner—approached the chapter board. She sat at the table during a meeting in our kitchen and ticked off the reasons to get involved: "This is not good use of land. It relies too much on cars. All those septic systems are resting on sand. The bird habitat is going." She was intense and earnest. Every day she slugged it out at the state capitol, proposing legislation, working on compromises, defending values that protected the natural world. She was right. The board agreed to host a forum to disseminate information about alternatives to residential development. Audubon had a reputation for reliable information.

Unlikely allies joined the chapter in hosting the forum: the Minnesota Farmers Union, hunting organizations, and the local snowmobile club among them. All of these groups required open space to make a living, to pursue their passions, or to enhance their members' lives. They saw no value in suburban development.

The land-use forum, the first public word spoken against the urbanization encroaching on North Branch, happened nearly a decade ago. It was deemed a great success for the large number of participants and the broad viewpoints expressed.

In the years following, I have often felt that the forum had no influence at all on the subsequent development of North Branch and Chisago County. The county's population has more than doubled in the past twenty-five years, and it is expected to double again by 2020. We will need twice as many schools, twice as much sewer and water capacity, twice as much of everything, just to keep up the level of services.

An environmentalist's urban sprawl is a developer's retirement plan. "Urban expansion" is perhaps a better term—the outward thrust of a metropolitan area that gobbles up land in large residential lots, strip mall commercial enterprises, and miles upon miles of paved-over earth. Although the phenomenon of urbanization seems straightforward, it is actually extremely complicated. Put any particular aspect under a magnifying lens to examine it, and you soon find yourself mired in a morass, where national and international policies, age-old attitudes toward land and nature, and changing ideas about what is valuable in life all play a part.

At its heart is the "farm crisis," the reality that our hardworking family farmers can no longer make a living from the land. Chisago County is, as usual, a microcosm of Minnesota: in the seven years bracketing Audubon's land-use forum, Chisago County lost sixteen farms, almost one-tenth of the state's total losses. Farms cease to be viable for complex reasons, among them low crop prices, high production costs, over-extension of debt, and government programs favoring large-scale farming—a potent, toxic brew spelling death to the midsized, diversified farming Chisago County once enjoyed. The human toll of the farm crisis is rife with anguish, depression, even suicide. Farm families are drained of their heritage as well as their identity. The empty barns with their weathered wood and sagging roof lines dotting our county's landscape are fitting emblems of the times.

At present we view this crisis in terms of trauma to human lives, but in truth a slower, broader emergency may be developing—the loss of productive land. As family farms grow houses as their final crop, we lose land that once supplied food for the nation. According to the American Farmland Trust, from 1982 to 1992 we lost about forty-six acres of farmland per hour, every day. Furthermore, the counties most threatened with development are those that produce the majority of the nation's food. How ironic that in an era when America's social pendulum has swung far to the "individualism" pole, we in Minnesota are losing our self-sufficiency in food production.

The devaluation of farming is only one part of the urbanization puzzle, however, as participants in the land-use forum soon discovered. Another aspect involves property taxes and the misconception that urban development decreases taxes. I had never thought carefully about everything that affects property taxes—and didn't really want to. But the topic is important because it drives sprawl. Local governments like the North Branch City Council could simply zone to keep out housing developments, but they don't. These government bodies need money to operate, and much of that money comes from property taxes. Since residential areas are taxed at a higher rate than agricultural land, people widely assumed that having more houses within city limits, or within county borders, lowers property taxes overall, because there are more taxpayers to share the burden.

Sounds reasonable, but it's not what residents experience. Each year when they tear open that tissue-thin letter from the county assessor, they see, unhappily, that taxes have gone up, again. So why isn't the theory working?

Again, numbers are important. In 1994, American Farmland Trust studied three communities in Minnesota which, like North Branch, are on the outer rings of urban development. The study looked at how much money new developments raised in taxes and how much it cost local communities to provide them with ambulance, fire and police protection, and other services. The study found that in each community housing developments cost much more money than their residents contributed in tax dollars. People in houses need fire and police protection, ambulance services, road maintenance, sewer and water lines (when the development is close enough to existing infrastructure), and, most costly of all, schools. The numbers look something like this: for every dollar raised by the residential sector, $1.07 was spent on services. Who subsidized the influx of new residents? We—the established residents—did!

Farmland, on the other hand, proved a bargain to local governments—for every dollar raised from agricultural land taxes, twenty-seven cents was spent on services. So, farmland was subsidizing development, too. Why didn't agricultural land need as many services? The snappy quip Auduboners like to toss is: "Cows don't go to school!"

The defining characteristic of urban sprawl is forced dependence on the automobile, made possible by the cheap price of gasoline. Despite what we think of as "high prices," gasoline is more affordable now than it has been in the past. In fact, adjusting for inflation, gas costs much less now than it did in the 1960s. This is significant because the vast majority of Chisago County's new residents commute to work in the Twin Cities each day. Housing developments are laid out so that people must take the car to go anywhere—to school, to the grocery store, to church. People are willing to drive everywhere because, at least on the surface, it doesn't seem costly to depend on the car. Houses tend to be more affordable way out on the sand plain, and newcomers often remark that they like "being out in the country."

. . . .

Years of pondering this complex phenomenon led me to identify three basic factors that encourage urban sprawl: a failure to value the family farm and policies that reflect this disregard, the misconception that development is fiscally desirable, and the cheap price of gas. Systems promoting sprawled development have been in place for decades. These factors go way beyond Chisago County's borders, and they are the reason there has been so little success in stemming the flood of new houses.

Twenty years ago on a trip to the East Coast, Tom and I found ourselves stranded in Concord, Massachusetts, in the late afternoon. We had dallied too long at Walden Pond and now, at rush hour, needed to drive thirty miles to a state forest, where we planned to camp overnight. Wishing to avoid the freeway carrying commuters out of Boston, we opted instead for a more direct route, a state highway which, our map told us, wound through several small towns with pleasant New England–sounding names like Bedford, Pinehurst, and Wilmington. We were midwesterners, unacquainted with the eastern seaboard.

Imagine our consternation, then, when we discovered that the thirty miles consisted of suburbs and stoplights, stop-and-go traffic that went on and on. We never saw any town center, we never reached any open land, we never viewed anything remotely resembling "country." This "scenic drive" took an hour and a half.

Is this Minnesota's future? The memory of our unhappy trip from Concord to North Reading returned to me on a recent fall afternoon as I drove across the Anoka Sand Plain from Chisago County to Elk River. Our future may have already arrived.

Most of the past decade's residential development in the North Branch area has occurred outside the reaches of city water and sewer. Each new house has its own septic system and well. The septic systems must meet the high standards set by Chisago County; they are not a worry at present. But each well is one more hole puncturing the bedrock overlaying the aquifer and, consequently, one more way for contaminants to seep into the water supply. Sand particles do not "cleanse" tainted rain as clay particles do, and the percolation rate through sand is swift.

The north branch of the Sunrise River was once so clean that a colleague of mine drove from the University of Minnesota to study its pristine water. It now has rising levels of phosphates and fecal coliform bacteria. Indeed, we greatly fear that it is only a matter of time before the water table underlying the sand plain is contaminated.

Lessening the threat of water contamination won't be easy. The pattern of development sprawled across the landscape on one- to five-acre lots presents a serious impediment to providing city services. Given the distance between houses, it is hard to see how North Branch, or any other sprawled community, will ever be able to hook up all its residents to city water and sewer. That same distance between houses makes it extremely difficult for Chisago County to maintain, plow, and sand roads. It's simply not cost effective.

The sand plain's signature oaks are victims of the rampant development. Oak wilt, a fungal disease that kills red oaks and sometimes bur oaks, infects trees with open wounds in the spring. The University of Minnesota Extension Program has held seminars for property owners on how to protect oak trees from wilt. Perhaps they should be targeting developers: spring is prime construction time, and trees are frequently injured in the process. I do not know of one developer who has altered construction schedules to protect the trees that heighten a property's appeal. Now in the spring when the oak woods green, there are telltale patches of brown amid the verdant canopy, the remains of trees that succumbed to wilt the previous summer.

Chisago County is losing its grassland birds as well. As agricultural land—particularly hayfields once used to feed dairy cows—gives way to houses, certain species lose habitat. As urbanization proceeds apace, western meadowlarks especially are in decline all around Minnesota. Fifteen years ago, I could hear both western and eastern meadowlarks singing in the open fields south of North Branch—interesting ecologically—but no longer. People often remark that their yards are filled with birds, but the birds they see are the ones common to groomed backyards all over North America—robins, blue jays, house finches, and English sparrows. Our native wild birds, like vesper and savannah sparrows, birds that won't show up at a feeder, are losing ground.

The North Branch schools, too, are affected, and not only by increased enrollment. Bus rides for some children take more than an hour for a distance that an individual car could cover in ten minutes. When high schoolers reach the age of sixteen, they get cars to circumvent these two-hour commutes. Bus ridership falls, and some services—the activity buses—are cancelled, making students participating in after-school sports or clubs totally dependent on the automobile.

In that they are like their parents. Mass transit, even by bus, will never be cost effective. Walking will never be an option. It is ironic that this kind of land use, often touted as providing consumers with choice—people choose to live in sprawled developments—actually puts constraints on their lives by confining them to their cars for hours each day.

Closing off options condemns our children to a future with limited choices. If we lose farmland close to the Twin Cities, the possibility of locally grown food shipped inexpensively to metro dwellers vanishes. If we develop land right up to the boundaries of Wild River Park, it can no longer expand to accommodate the Twin Cities visitors whose numbers are expected to double in the next twenty years.

All of these issues are sober, realistic reasons to halt this wasteful pattern of land use. But they seem feeble somehow. They do not truly speak to the heart of the matter.

After our congested drive through Massachusetts, we crossed the border into New Hampshire and gradually put distance between us and the greater Boston area. Granite outcroppings and craggy white pines loomed out of the earth. Small patches of wildness existed. We felt we had room to breathe once more.

My heartache as a child, watching Roseville's last bit of untamed land disappear, I now believe was rooted in the intuitive sense that something was off kilter. The human presence was growing too large and squeezing the rest of creation into ever-decreasing pockets. No more marshes for turtles, no more fields for gophers, no more breathing room. However occupied agricultural land is—and the human hand lays heavy upon it—there is still room at the margins for other forms of life. The land is still open to possibility.

We may wrap ourselves in "property rights" and claim the freedom of private ownership, but these statements beg the question: exactly what is it that we are free to own? Can we really possess a living entity?

Urban sprawl is merely hundreds of small-scale versions of the nineteenth century's westward expansion, the taming and eradication of North America's natural world. Of that phenomenon, the ecologist Aldo Leopold wrote, "Man always kills the thing he loves, and so we the pioneers have killed our wilderness. . . . I am glad I shall never be young without wild country to be young in. Of what avail are 40 freedoms without a blank spot on the map?"

We have yet to answer that question.

Flooding, Forgetting, and Remembering

THE ARROWHEAD RESTS IN MY PALM. The piece is thin, with slightly scalloped edges created by a small, sharp tool. Slender, milky lines traverse the smoky agate from which it was chiseled. Deceptively fragile, the one-inch specimen would easily penetrate the thick hide of a white-tailed deer. It is a work of art.

The arrowhead's owners, Anne and Loring Olson, produced this beautiful piece when I queried them about Indian artifacts discovered on their farm. Anne had come upon the arrowhead one day while working in her garden, a genuine treasure buried in the sandy soil.

The arrowhead wasn't entirely unexpected. The Olson farm, located on the northeastern shore of Goose Lake in northern Chisago County, has been a gold mine for arrowheads. The field south of the barn is especially bountiful. A previous owner filled an old cigar box with the ancient artifacts. She also found an intact tomahawk with a sturdy stone head and a carved wooden handle, strips of rawhide still wrapping the stone to the wood. Perhaps a battle on the shores of Goose Lake accounted for the heavy deposit of arrowheads. A peaceful explanation is more likely, though: years of residency on the "narrows" separating upper and lower Goose Lake, a well-documented site of a long-occupied Ojibwe village. State archaeologists have discovered a cemetery on the Olson farm as well.

The lovely little arrowhead, with its translucent pearly color, is remarkable for more than its beauty. It embodies a culture. It tells me that people much different from me once called Chisago County home.

One hundred and fifty years after the Ojibwe who fashioned those tools were the dominant culture in Chisago County, the community of North Branch is caught in the convulsive throes of rapid population growth. Because the town is situated only forty-five miles from the economically robust Twin Cities and because it has ready access to an interstate highway, North Branch has been a magnet to developers seeking to build suburban tract housing. Houses are spreading over the sand plain. North Branch's population has nearly tripled in the last twenty years.

There is a heavy cost to urbanization, and not all losses can be measured in dollars and cents. People see the new AmericInn and Kentucky Fried Chicken franchises and worry about becoming "just like everyone else." As the oak trees come down or wither from oak wilt, as the last prairie grass fringes are replaced by bluegrass, as farmsteads that have served as landmarks for over a century disappear, there is a sense that history itself is evaporating. The natural world, the various recountings of the people who have lived their lives in North Branch, their buildings, their craft—all these contribute to a sense of place, convincing residents that this community, situated on the north branch of the Sunrise River, is a special patch of earth.

Far from an exercise in nostalgia, identifying a place is actually a form of truth telling. Every community is unique, beginning with its latitude and longitude, which define its sunrises and sunsets and, to a large extent, its weather. Its location is responsible for the angle of the sun, which in turn affects how quickly roads become ice-free in winter, how shadows fall and shade yards and gardens, whether or not the air warms in midsummer. Until the advent of the automobile, people were intimately aware of their surroundings, mainly because they walked or used horses to get from one place to another. At the slow pace of a measured step, it is easy to see the texture of the soil or the potato plants in flower, to spy the red berries of native plants, to hear the rustle of leaves or the murmur of wind through big bluestem. It wasn't necessary to consciously identify the subtleties of home for North Branchers of the past—they knew it in their bones. Now, with car travel making it possible to live in multiple locations each day, the intimacy with which we once knew home has become rare.

An understanding of history is life enhancing. When I recall the other people who once called North Branch home, I gain a truer perspective on my own place in the greater scheme of things. As I imagine an Ojibwe family enduring a bitterly cold January night in a wigwam, I appreciate the central heating of my own home all the more. The joyous Fourth of July celebrations of the early Yankee settlers call to mind the great age of the United States and how long we have valued our country. I suddenly see myself as a small ripple in the great stream of people who have flowed into and out of Chisago County, and I become aware that other North Branchers will come after me. What will our present community bequeath them?

It is axiomatic that the past becomes the future, and yet North Branch, like many places, has a pattern of forgetting its history. Each time a tide of people has swept into the sand plain, it has swamped what existed before.

Although archaeological knowledge of the Anoka Sand Plain is incomplete, research suggests that the region has been inhabited for ten to eleven thousand years. A succession of American Indian groups of differing cultural traditions occupied what is now Chisago County, hunting bison, fishing in the many lakes, and, in more recent times, harvesting wild rice. The last of the native groups, the Ojibwe, moved into the sand plain region from Lake Superior about three hundred years ago. They left behind the arrowheads and the perfectly preserved tomahawk on the shores of Goose Lake.

Most reminders of the Ojibwe community were erased, however, by the advent of Euro-American settlement in Chisago County. Following the treaty of 1837 between the United States and the Ojibwe, Euro-Americans flowed into the area to work in the logging industry, to set up shop in newly forming towns, or to farm. Most of the early white settlers were from the East Coast, bearing Yankee names like "Ingalls" or "Pratt." Many were from upstate New York. The Americans cleared the forests and broke the virgin sod, obliterating Ojibwe hunting grounds. Ojibwe settlements were abandoned as the native people felt pressured to leave the area. A Chisago County history book notes that the white settlers were the first to cultivate the soil in Chisago County—a likely erroneous claim, since the Ojibwe were known to grow both corn and beans, particularly on flood plains. Today's residents regularly pass Indian burial mounds in blissful ignorance of their presence. (The mounds remain unidentified, primarily to prevent artifact seekers from defiling them.) The first people have been forgotten—save for a small agate arrowhead.

The next great migration of people into Chisago County came a few decades later, when Swedes left their homeland in a swelling tide to escape years of crop failures and starvation. A handful of Swedes arrived in the county in 1851, but the peak influx occurred in the 1880s. When it had subsided, Chisago County was hailed as "Swede County," with one-third of its residents claiming Swedish origins in 1896. By the turn of the century, the East Coast names of "Wilkes," "Smith," and "McCutcheon" had been replaced by "Oleson," "Swenson," and "Lindstrom." The Episcopalian and Congregational churches closed as the Swedish Lutheran congregation

POTATO CITY

expanded. The pietistic Swedes promoted a ban on the sale of alcohol and led the county's temperance movement. North Branch—once a distribution center for the Schmidt Brewing Company—went dry before prohibition became federal law.

Each wave of immigrants inundates the past. "The majority of the early settlers in this area were Swedish," proclaims another history book of North Branch. The Yankee names on the oldest headstones in Oak Hill Cemetery have been scoured nearly smooth.

Like the Swedish immigration, the coming of a commuter populace began slowly and extended over several decades. North Branch's population grew in the 1960s, even before the freeway was completed. But the stunning, rapid growth—the flood—has occurred only in the last ten years. North Branch is still in the process of sorting out the changes, but the forgetting has already begun. Who remembers the festive Midsummer's Day picnics in Elmgren's Grove, or the fourteen warehouses flanking the railroad tracks and what they stored? What of the Swedes will be remembered, what will be discarded?

Members of these newest waves, however, are unlike the previous immigrants in that they do not traverse the sand plain on foot. Indeed, travel by necessity is almost entirely by automobile, the scents and sounds blocked out, the scenery blurred. Moving about under the power of a gasoline-combustion engine, the most immediate world is the car's interior, which doesn't change as people move between latitudes and longitudes. If most of one's time is spent away from the house, where exactly is home? Is it possible that the next generation of North Branchers won't have a sense of place? Or even a sense of community?

Living in a car subtly threatens one's humanity. Zipping back and forth over asphalt, tussling with traffic lights and entrance ramps, we forget that we, the drivers of automobiles, are creatures of the earth. We overlook the fact that we are utterly dependent on the planet's succor—the freshness of its water, the fertility of its soil, the warmth of the sun. It is equally easy to forget that we are all members of a community, reliant on the honesty and good will of our neighbors, the effectiveness of the school system, and the stability of local businesses. We cease to be humans, being, and become, instead, merely humans, driving.

Yet I am hopeful that this most recent flood of newcomers will not entirely swamp North Branch's sense of identity. Even as developers attempt to erase the talismans of our past, I have witnessed a renewed interest in what has gone before. North Branch sixth graders study a unit on local history, so every middle-school student knows a little bit about potato farming, the importance of the railroad, and Swedish immigration. When the railroad bed was converted to a bicycle trail several years ago, it was dedicated as the "Sunrise Prairie Trail," a tribute to the significance of the river and the native prairie grasses. The local community education program has undertaken a project of interviewing older residents and recording their stories. And the North Branch Chamber of Commerce recently set up a website featuring a short history of the community, complete with evocative photos of potato farmers and others of the past.

All of these are effective ways to remember who we are. Like the little agate arrowhead from Goose Lake, they remind us that we were not the first people here, and we will not be the last. We will leave our legacy, but much of what we do will be forgotten—or rewritten—by those who replace us.

Four

The Sunrise River

THE SUNRISE RIVER cuts through the heart of Chisago County, separating sand from the richer glacial till of the Chisago Lakes and Taylors Falls area. It marks the division of two plant communities—the oak savanna of the sand plain and the maple basswood forest of the Grantsburg till plain. Whole human settlements have taken their identity and their economy from these two ecosystems: North Branch wealthy with sand-loving potatoes; Chisago City, Lindstrom, and Center City renowned for their glacier-formed lakes.

The living border of the river's south branch approximates the southern shoreline of the long-ago glacial lake, formed from melt water of the last glacier. The glacier bequeathed a different legacy of substrate on each side of the river, and dissimilar soils, with different capacities to sustain crops, have formed. The quality of the landscape changes dramatically as one crosses the river.

Despite a century of "progress" that tore open the sod of its watershed, planted factories on its banks, and logged off the virgin forest, the little river has remained remarkably pristine. Its waters have been clear, harboring fish species that are indicators of clean water. Sadly, in the last decade rapid urbanization has taken its toll, and phosphate contamination now threatens the river's clarity.

There are two upper forks to the Sunrise. The northern arm rises from a wetlands west of its namesake town, North Branch, and flows eastward. The southern arm also flows out of a wetlands, just south of the county's southern border. Over the last century, this wetlands has been under siege; in the last five years, it has been threatened with obliteration.

The amorphous beginnings of Chisago County's Sunrise River work against its identification as the natural organizing feature around which all others revolve. Worse, a lack of recognizable beginning encourages people to overlook the river altogether. A headwaters is significant: what would the upper reaches of the Mississippi be without Lake Itasca?

Crossing the Sunrise on one of several bridges is a daily act for many residents, but few actually have contact with its waters. One May morning several years ago, our local Audubon chapter dropped canoes into the river. Our goal: paddle downstream to its confluence with the larger St. Croix. Wild River Audubon has for years assumed care for a segment of the river in the state-organized Adopt-a-River program. Once a year, members of our chapter walk its banks or ply its waters, picking up trash, hauling out old tires, and removing odds and ends, artifacts that detract from its pristine nature.

On this Saturday, it was nearly summer. A string of hot days earlier in the month had quickened spring's leisurely course. Trees were in full leaf, and the steep banks of the narrow waterway were lush with new growth. It was a sunny day, a sparkling day. Birds were everywhere—rose-breasted grosbeaks, red-eyed vireos, orioles and flycatchers, and many, many warblers. Maple, box-elder, oak, and ash boughs formed a verdant bower over the water, dappling the shady recesses with sunlight.

By midsummer the Sunrise is too dry to canoe, but in May the water level is high enough to provide paddlers with challenge and delight. The current is swift and lively; riffles and bubbling rapids break the surface at intervals, and paddlers are required to be alert. No one maintains this waterway for canoeists, and trees frequently fall across the river and lodge perpendicular to the current, becoming "sweepers." A swift current will quickly carry a canoe up against a sweeper if the paddlers do not act decisively to circumvent it. Once the canoe aligns itself parallel to the tree, it is often too late to prevent swamping. With water pushing relentlessly against its flank, the canoe becomes unstable and tips, spilling its occupants. All of this happens in a matter of seconds.

The first canoe in our party swamped in this manner within our first hour on the river. Without warning, our venerable president, Dayle, and a new recruit to the chapter—whom we had hoped, alas, to impress—were in the water and sputtering, clinging to the willows that swept in from the banks. The rest of us, witnessing this split-second event, were taken aback—no one had expected to go for a dip that morning. But it was hard to be strongly disturbed with the air warm and the sunshine full on the water. We helped the wet ones retrieve their canoe and accessories and continued downstream.

The sweepers were everywhere. Paddling stern in our canoe, Tom avoided one after another with skillful paddling, quick thinking, and brute strength, until a low-slung box-elder got the best of us. The river drew our canoe toward the tree's upper branches, and the stern swung drunkenly inward and began the destabilizing rocking. I glanced backward to see what measures Tom might be taking to pull us out of our predicament and, to my astonishment, discovered he was no longer in the canoe. In fact, he was nowhere to be seen! Only his canvas fedora floated on the river's surface.

Events happen quickly on a swiftly flowing river. Before I could wonder where he was, Tom came bobbing to the surface, his head reclaiming the hat as he emerged. While I had been tussling with the box-elder's crown, he had stepped out of the canoe in an attempt to stabilize it, thinking the water only a few feet deep. What a surprise to find that it was over his head! He remained in the river, swimming alongside the canoe as together we eased the craft around the sweeper and guided it once more to the unimpeded stream.

Cleaning the river from a canoe requires both skill in paddling and judgment. It is easy to spot discarded trash: five-gallon pails and twisted chrome bumpers are blights on the land that scream to our eyes. It is another thing altogether to maneuver a canoe to the proper location: it almost always involves paddling desperately upstream, clinging to bits of dry marsh grass on the riverbank to maintain position, then leaning precariously far from the center of the canoe to reach for the dented beer can that is always just barely at one's fingertips.

Some years, the junk we scavenge is remarkable. Old tires, lodged stubbornly in river muck, are common. Half-filled oil drums—leaking—are more rare and hard to pull into a wobbling canoe (although it has been done). Mostly, we take in plastic bags and crumpled beer cans. The most interesting item on this day's paddle was an old yellow raincoat, probably lost when a day-tripper's canoe overturned on a tricky stretch upstream.

Despite its beauty and its relatively clean condition this spring, the Sunrise River is in trouble, for little of the river is protected from development. We fear it is only a matter of time before the landowners that now maintain the riverbank in its natural state succumb to the load of ever-increasing taxes or the lure of developers' dollars and sell off lots for houses with river views. Most of the landowners cherish the river as we do, and the county has setback requirements that protect the bank somewhat, but we know from painful experience that when development fever hits, nothing is sacred.

These gloomy thoughts threatened to mar a sunny May morning, but I resolutely put them from my mind. I frequently worry too much, forgetting that we live in the present as well as for the future. As we paused for a break in a quiet backwater, locking arms and legs over the gunwales so that we all hung together, I merely basked in the warmth of sun and friendship. On this day, we were in our prime, strong and happy. The full flush of spring surrounded us, birds singing and tender green leaves glowing in sunlight. Maybe we cannot save this river. But on this morning the waters were clean, the banks were forested, and songbirds, those bright jewels, were everywhere.

It is April. We Auduboners are older, but again we gather at the river, one of our enduring rites of spring. This year, as in the past five, we are observing Earth Day by cleaning up an old dump along the banks of the Sunrise. We no longer hold a chapter-wide river cleanup conducted from canoes. The sweepers, and the prospect of a lawsuit should inexperienced canoeists capsize, have made us wary. We continue to canoe the river in parties of two or three, cleaning as we go, but we do not advertise it as a chapter-sponsored event.

In the past, the dumps have been extensive. We worked on one for two consecutive Aprils, the first year pulling large items up the riverbank with chain and winch, the second rooting out smaller items that the soil was already reclaiming. The large items were memorable: half a car, two or three beds, an old gas stove, several refrigerators.

One of the refrigerators almost killed me. I was at the bottom of the hill as it was being hauled out. When the apparatus connecting it to the winch came undone, it tumbled tail over teakettle toward me. Misjudging its acceleration, I watched with interest as it headed my way. The men on the hill above me had a more accurate view of the scene and froze in horror as I slowly sauntered away. At the last moment, suddenly apprehending it was traveling much faster than I realized, I scrambled to safety with inches to spare.

But there are no refrigerators in this dump. We see only old cans and pails peeking out from last year's leaf litter.

The morning is fresh and sunny but cool around the edges. The rising sun's rays filter through white pine boughs, their needles refracting the rays into long, yellow streaks. Fuzzy-stemmed hepatica, lavender flowers still curled in sleep, poke out from the duff. Here and there, we see early bloodroots, the white waxy flowers like miniature tulips, closed tightly. Below us, the Sunrise River runs swiftly on to meet the St. Croix. In the early morning light, the water takes on the color of the surrounding banks, a translucent blend of browns and greens.

One of our Auduboners organizes the Adopt-a River cleanup each year. Gary arranges for a garbage hauling firm to provide a dumpster, trash containers, and several able-bodied men to help us. He also brings in other volunteer groups, like a local Boy Scout troop and the auxiliary of Wild River State Park, which borders part of the Sunrise. Our Audubon chapter can use the help: only six of us have shown up this morning. The responsibilities of mid-life—work and family—claim more of our time now than they did five years ago. Plus, I admit to myself as I grab a garbage bag and ease down the steep, brambled bank, we're all beginning to show signs of battle fatigue. Rapid urban development sprawling out from the Twin Cities assaults the environment in many ways. The numerous problems all require focused attention. We're becoming exhausted.

Gary enjoys working through these official agencies, set up to provide society with so-called "environmental services." He has to: in his job as county recycling coordinator, they're his bread and butter. He's good at what he does, and through his grant writing he brings in money to provide additional "environmental services" for county residents. Today he has coordinated the help of a privately owned garbage service and a variety of civic groups to clean up the riverbanks.

I suppose these "environmental services" are necessary. After all, if we didn't regulate setbacks along shorelines, the open burning of garbage, or residential septic systems, the place would be a mess. Their chief drawback lies in the false impression they give that the government—and that would be us—is interested in addressing our environmental woes, that these relatively Band-Aid actions will be sufficient to pull us out of the downward spiral of environmental decline.

So here we are on Earth Day, picking up a dump, a nice, politically safe activity. From the physical perspective, however, it may not be so safe. As I survey the scene at my feet, I begin to think about tetanus shots. The dump is so old that the cans are thoroughly rusted, no longer identifiable by brand name, except for a handful of faded, one-pound Maxwell House coffee tins. Everything has settled into the soil. We unearth odd-looking jars, a blue milk of magnesia container, and some soda bottles. Every glass item has a hole in it; someone speculates that a kid had a great time with a pellet gun one day. We fill buckets and bags and lug them over to a large trash container that will be hauled up the steep riverbank to the waiting dumpster.

It is pleasant to be on the banks of the Sunrise on this dewy spring morning. Liquidy river sounds provide background to our idle chat as we move along like cotton pickers over the ground, stashing rusted trash in our bags. We admire the hepatica, listen for yellow-rumped warblers, catch up on our lives.

The active members of Wild River Audubon are a close-knit group. There are so few of us and problems are so great that we forged firm friendships long ago. My friends don't seem as concerned as me that we are diddling away Earth Day, picking up cans. They are merely happy to be here. In this, I reflect later, they are the wiser. They know that you can't save the earth in one grand gesture, that only small, persistent, repetitive action by everyone will make a difference. They know that the real Earth Day gesture isn't cleaning up a dump but simply being present—out in the sunshine, grubbing in the dirt, attending to the river.

The world is lovely, fresh, and renewing. It would speak to us. Are we listening?

One Seed at a Time

ON A CLEAR JUNE DAY, the oak savanna at Wild River State Park is fresh with color and alive with birdsong. Buttery yellow Carolina puccoon and bold magenta prairie phlox enliven the wispy grasses. Dusty oaks provide shade singly or in clusters. The dry trill of a savannah sparrow drifts out over the grasses. I pick my way through poison ivy, seeking something rare: wild lupine.

Wild lupine is a robust, shin-high plant with green whorls of leaves that splay out like little hands. In mid-June its showy blue flowers are at peak bloom, and where they grow, a profusion of blues and violets meets my eye. A classic savanna plant, lupine is at home on sandy soil, thriving amid prairie grasses and in the partial shade of oaks. When Wild River's oak savanna was partially cleared for cultivation and pasture, wild lupine was one of the casualties. Delectable to cattle, this once common plant was nearly eaten out of existence.

. . . .

Wild River State Park, where I am collecting the seed, is on the far eastern edge of the Anoka Sand Plain. In the 150 years since European settlement, the land now protected in the park has been logged, cleared, farmed, and abandoned. A site on the St. Croix River, which forms the park's eastern border, was eyed for a hydroelectric dam around 1925. Had the dam been constructed, a large portion of the park would have been submerged. But the sand saved the river valley from inundation: engineers could not find sufficient bedrock to anchor a dam large enough for the power company's needs. The company transferred the land to the State of Minnesota in the 1970s for use as a park. Its charter expressly states that the park should be managed to preserve its natural ecosystem.

Wild River is most fortunate to have park naturalist Dave Crawford looking out for its native residents. Tall, toothpick-thin, sporting a bushy, reddish beard, Dave arrived at the park ten years ago with a keen understanding of native plant communities and a special passion for prairies that had been whetted during his student days at the University of Minnesota. His pale eyes kindle behind wire-rimmed glasses as he describes how his love of plants began: "I did well in [Dr. Morley's Minnesota Plant Life] class, so he called me and offered me a job as a teaching assistant, which was the first time anyone ever called and *offered* me a job! It was great!"

After college, walking railroad rights of way adjacent to his home and discovering remnant prairie plants clinging to life on those narrow strips of land further fanned the flames. When Dave took the position of naturalist at Wild River, his trained botanical eye spotted the presence of old, broad-canopied bur oaks hunkered down in the midst of the park's brushy oak woodlands. Bur oaks are often the telltale indicators of past savannas. Trees that grow up with elbowroom in a savanna assume a different shape than those that mature in the competitive conditions of a forest. Savanna oaks form wide, spreading crowns and heavy lower limbs, while woodland oaks are slender and less robust.

Dave understood that the presence of widely spaced bur oaks indicated a savanna once grew on the land now claimed by aspen and pin oak. Hearsay from landowners who had farmed within the park's boundaries supported this interpretation, as did analysis of the U.S. government land survey from 1839. Armed with the historical record, as well as with what his eyes could see, Dave, along with park manager Chuck Kartak, embarked on a course of action to re-establish the natural conditions that create a savanna.

Before the arrival of Europeans, fire had shaped the landscape, favoring bur oaks and prairie plant species that could survive and even flourish after burning. Fires were caused by lightning strikes or were set by native people, who used them to clear away brush and to promote growth of grasses that attracted wildlife. Suppression of fires, the intuitive response of European settlers, allowed "weedy species," those that wouldn't be found on a savanna, to spring up and change the complexion of the landscape.

As a first step toward restoring a savanna, Dave and the park staff cut down invasive species—prickly ash, hazel, aspen—that had emerged where natural fire had been suppressed. In successive years, they used prescribed burning to keep brush at bay. They soon found that these cosmetic actions were hardly enough to encourage a healthy, diverse plant community. In some areas that had been pasture, grazing cattle had cropped choice plants so persistently that no traces remained—not existing roots, not even seeds lying dormant in the soil.

Dave wanted to re-introduce plants that had been lost in these former pasturelands and to boost the number of species that ought to be growing in less damaged areas of the park. He put together a plan using volunteers to canvass existing plants and collect seeds to be sown in the impoverished areas. The plan began modestly: native grasses, like big and little bluestem and Indian grass, were harvested for their seed, which was scattered the next spring in large, open fields that had been pre-treated to rid them of non-native plants. That was the start of a prairie, one step in restoring a savanna.

However, Dave was really interested in the less abundant, broad-leaved plants—the ones producing colorful flowers, like the

---

fuchsia of blazing star and the canary yellow of Carolina puccoon. The vibrant color and intricacy of these prairie flowers makes nature lovers' hearts beat a little faster. Moreover, apart from aesthetic appeal, a richly diverse plant community seems to do better during droughts and other periods of stress. Promoting the growth of many native species in a restored savanna actually enhances its stability in an ever-changing world.

For these broad-leaved plants, Dave selected several fairly common species, photocopied illustrations of their seed heads, and turned loose volunteers toting ice cream buckets, directing them to places in the park where he had spotted plants. On one of these early collecting trips, I was handed a brittle brown sprig of white prairie clover and told that he'd seen some growing "west of the bridge over Dry Creek, on the tiny prairie patch next to the path below the visitors' center."

That was seven years ago. Since then, through trial and error and enhanced publicity, Dave's program has blossomed into an effort involving over two hundred volunteers collecting 150 species. "Still not a prairie," he notes, "but a very good approximation."

In the ongoing project to restore Wild River's oak savanna, park managers have targeted lupine as one of the prairie flowers to bring back. It grows in only a few areas in the park but could probably do well in many other spots. It needs a steward, and I am assigned to monitor and assist it. I need to locate the plants, record the progress of flowers, seeds, and pods, and, finally, harvest the seeds.

Lupine grows in places that receive shade part of the day. The park's remnant population can be found near the main road, in open areas, under the shadows cast by bur oaks. My first time out, I have no trouble spotting the plants even though they have not yet begun to bloom. Arriving to monitor their progress several weeks later, I see that they share their space with large clumps of poison ivy—a significant piece of information that had not been obvious on my prior visit. Now, with the lupine bearing striking blue flowers, I pick my path carefully from cluster to cluster. My policy with poison ivy plants is similar to my policy with snakes: leave them alone.

Lupine produces seeds in mid-summer. I clip the swollen seed-pods and store them in paper sacks to be "processed" later on in the nature center. They'll be "de-podded," as one would shell garden peas (which are relatives to lupine), and picked over to remove debris.

But Dave has another task for me. Late in June, he hands me a small manila envelope weighted by several handfuls of last summer's seed—about $250 worth. The seeds are white, pebble-like, about the size of split peas. "Just scatter them in somewhat open areas where you think lupine might grow," he tells me. "Don't fuss too much—it should be fun." Compulsive gardener that I am, I seek out pocket gopher mounds in sandy earth along the margins of wood-land and grassy openings. I plant the seeds and carefully pat soil over them. My efforts are rewarded two weeks later when the smallest of seedlings, sporting tiny green whorls of leaves, poke through the soil. The lupine population increases.

The spread of wild lupine has consequences for a butterfly with a finicky appetite. Karner blues inhabit sandy pine or oak prairies and lakeshore dunes, where wild lupine is the sole host for their voracious caterpillars. Adult butterflies are small, their delicate cerulean wings marked with orange marginal spots. Karner blues are rare and considered endangered.

There are many species and subspecies of butterflies designated as "blues." The group in general is a challenge to classify, for there are many types, and the differences between them are slight and variable. They present an intricate intellectual puzzle that the writer—and butterfly expert—Vladimir Nabokov undertook to master; my Peterson's *A Field Guide to the Butterflies* credits him for his "very thorough work." Karners are actually a subspecies of Melissa blues. These little butterflies tend to congregate at mud puddles, sometimes by the hundreds.

Karner blues do not inhabit Wild River State Park, but they do have a breeding population twenty miles north, at Wisconsin's

Crex Meadows Wildlife Area. The habitat is right for Karner blues at Wild River, and they probably once lived here, so when I sow my seeds, I walk north, consciously trying to bring the lupine population closer to Crex Meadows. I now watch for the flutter of blue wings, for a fleeting glimpse of azure at damp spots or over meadows. We are waiting for a wandering Karner blue to rediscover Minnesota.

Ah, the energy at Wild River State Park: leaping flames tended by trained burn crews, volunteers with collection pails, more volunteers to pick and clean the collected seed over the winter, still more volunteers to sow it in the spring. With all the hand-collected seed gathered over a decade, Wild River State Park has gained about two hundred acres of replanted prairie—two hundred acres in ten years. It's a postage stamp on the broad face of the planet. And it's just stage one of re-establishing a savanna.

In stage two, oaks will be reintroduced, probably by way of acorns sprouting into seedlings, then maturing into saplings, slowly, slowly becoming larger. After the oaks will come plants that shun the full sun of a prairie but thrive in partial shade—woodland species providing the mix that makes a savanna unique in diversity and plant structure. None of us involved in the restoration will live to see good savanna growing in the park. It will take longer than a human lifetime.

Dry-eyed critics have leveled charges at meticulous restoration efforts like Wild River's, claiming they are little more than nostalgic attempts to bring back an Eden that vanished with the invasion of European settlers. They say it is simply arbitrary to champion one type of ecosystem over another.

Biologists involved in restoration counter this charge by pointing out that their efforts are directed toward supplying an environmental force—like frequent fire—and not a specific landscape. The heroic work of seed collectors has an endpoint: their main function at present is to restore plant diversity, but at some future juncture their work will be done. Then we will see if the savanna can maintain itself under the evolutionary conditions of disturbance by fire.

Still, are we sentimentalists, grooming a personal–though wild–garden? Wouldn't our energies be better directed toward something really necessary for a healthy environment–such as persistently pestering our legislators to produce a sustainable energy policy or addressing a consumer culture whose excesses cause a plethora of environmental woes?

I ponder these criticisms when I'm out in the field. Rather than activist endeavors, my thoughts turn to houses. The word "ecology" comes from the Greek oikos, meaning "house," so I'm not completely off track. Let's say I have a lovely, beautifully furnished house. One day, while I'm away, someone has a wild party in the house and utterly trashes it–carpet stained, mirrors smashed, furniture broken. It is no longer fully functional or beautiful, but the roof is intact; it still keeps out the rain. Is it sentimental to think that I ought to restore my house to its former condition?

The answer depends on the direction I am looking, forward or backward. If my aim in restoration is to recreate the house to the last detail in order to relive happy past moments–birthdays, Christmases–then it might be a sentimental effort.

But what if my aim is to enrich my future life: to recreate beauty and functionality and to provide a worthy inheritance for my children? Is that sentimental?

What about the small furnishings? A china figurine–well, I wouldn't really need that. But a cell phone on the nightstand, to use in case of fire? That might save the house.

Like all analogies, mine has limitations. But the small items that might or might not be important are interesting, because ecologists will tell you that we don't understand any ecosystem well enough to determine whether we can get along without all the details. We know that ecosystems with a high level of biodiversity recover more quickly from disturbances like drought, but we don't know which species are essential to the ecosystem and which ones won't be missed if they go extinct. This lack of knowledge makes our efforts at Wild River seem less like paging through a yellowed photo album and more like sitting at a roulette table, trying to calculate how much we can afford to lose.

In my gloomy moments, I wonder if the charge of sentimentalism is, in truth, a refusal to come to terms with the loss of North America's wealth of life and a rejection of any guilt in our collective abuse of the land. Yet when I am at work on the nascent savanna, gloom and guilt do not exist. What I see is fresh and bountiful—big bluestem grass dripping with seed, dried lupine pods swollen with promise. The earth is incredibly lavish in its production of new life. Taking my cue from nature, I see that each new spring brings possibility. The hope it engenders ties us to the bountiful oaks adorned with May's catkins, to every savannah sparrow pioneering restored land.

Bringing It Back

THE SEPTEMBER SUN IS WARM ON MY BACK as I bend over the dried remnants of asters dotting a tiny patch of field at Wild River State Park. I am collecting ripe seed from azure asters for the park's Prairie Care Program, depositing it into a cavernous five-quart ice cream bucket. The asters are only two feet high, so I work in a crouched position. The seed heads are small, about half an inch in diameter, tawny bits of nothing weighing less than a postage stamp. They harbor the first seeds I've collected from asters I've been observing for more than a month. Some of the azures are still blooming, their delicate violet-blue blossoms vivid amid the browning grasses.

Although I could feel virtuous performing this volunteer work, it is in truth demoralizing. The yield from each plant is so meager that my efforts seem futile. I will never fill half a pail, that much is clear. And there is no aesthetic appeal to the work. When I peer into my bucket, the downy refuse I have collected appears unlovely—

dull, colorless, vegetative bits, wholly different from the rounded, glistening reds and blues of the berries that usually fill my collecting pails.

My middle-aged back is complaining. My rounded shoulders, the curved vertebral column leave their mark on my muscles. I rise to stretch, gazing out over the park to the southwest, where an afternoon sun glows benignly. The landscape before me is a hodge-podge of plant forms: oak woods stand beyond the road bordering the campground, but a fringe of non-native scotch pine hems its edges. A large expanse of restored "prairie"—a nearly pure patch of Indian grass, really—lies before me, but wood lots flank it on every side. Quaking aspen, the supreme weed of cutover woods, fringe the patchy oak stands. It looks like nothing ecologically classifiable. It looks like damaged land.

Still, it pleases me. The oaks are green, their leaves clattering softly as drafts of air puff through them. The dried grasses smell like hay, sweet and warm. From time to time, a cabal of crows croaks overhead. My eyes sweep over the openness, and its expansiveness transfers a bit of ease to my mind. I turn back to my work.

Tom has come with me to collect today. It is a rare, unscheduled Saturday for him, and he is pleased at the chance to be outside, doing useful, restorative work. He has wandered off to the north, out of conversation range, so what might have been a shared activity with laughter and small talk has become an individual pursuit. We are on our own with our individual thoughts, which are given free rein by the mindless, repetitive action. I do my best thinking with this type of work. I mull over petty problems, rewrite essays in my mind, and plan courses of action to address nagging worries.

My fingers bend the dried asters and gently tug at the fluff attached to the seeds. I remember "The Six Swans," the Brothers Grimm fairy tale that I read to my daughter last night. In it, the one sibling not changed by the wicked stepmother into a swan needs to collect aster down in order to liberate her six hexed brothers. She gathers the down, cards and spins it, weaves it into cloth, and sews six magical shirts. At the proper moment, the shirts will be tossed over the heads of the swan-brothers, and they will transform into human beings again.

Why did the storytellers choose aster down? What experience did they have with this scarce, filmy fluff? It intrigues me to think of gathering aster down as transforming work. How will my worries transform under the mild monotony of my seed collecting? Will they become something new? Will I become something different? Perhaps I am collecting more than seeds today. Maybe I am collecting thoughts as well as seeds, thoughts that now need to be cured and shelved to await the proper time for sowing, when they will sprout and bear fruit.

I volunteer as a Prairie Care Species Steward in the effort to restore oak savanna at Wild River State Park. In the past, I monitored wild lupine, a fairly easy species to locate and harvest. But now I was assigned two species of aster: the azure (*Aster oolentangiensis*) and the heath (*Aster ericoides*). My task was the same as for lupine: observe existing stands, look for new, unrecorded plants, collect data on when they blossomed, set seed, and ripened, and, later, collect the seed to be sown the following spring. Park naturalist Dave Crawford handed me laminated sheets about each species with photos of the plants in flower, growing in the field, and dried, as an herbarium specimen. When I turned the sheets over, I found maps—aerial photos—of the park, with known locations of each species highlighted in yellow. A third laminated sheet showed diversity "hot spots"—places that harbored a high number of different prairie species.

One might think that, armed with this much information, the task ahead would be a snap. When Dave handed me my sheets and I saw my assignment, though, I admit to experiencing faint-heartedness. As a zoologist, I had not been trained in the finer points of the aster family—a large and confusing group. Minnesota has dozens of different asters, all of them looking much like small daisies. I wasn't reassured, either, when a botanist friend working at a nearby table looked up from her microscope to tell me that azures "look brighter than other asters" and heaths "form masses of white in bloom." What is "brighter?" How could I tell? Other asters were white. Would they also look like a mass?

With diligence, however, I located all the known sites of my two asters even before they came into bloom. As late summer mellowed into the gold of September, the asters produced flowers, first the azure's brilliant blue, then the heath's frothy white wands, comprised of the tiniest leaves and flowers. Each week I trekked to the park and recorded their progress: "blooming," "blooms fading," "starting to brown," "seeds present but not ripe." Each week the oaks were slightly duller, the grasses less green. The warblers from the far north passed through the park in dull fall plumage, on their way to Central America, and the oak woods grew quiet. Finally, the asters were brown and fuzzy with seed, and I had only memories of the past summer.

When, at last, the seeds were ripe and their downy tufts could be plucked without leaving the seed behind, I reached for the empty ice cream buckets. It was time to collect.

Biologists estimate that one-tenth of the state of Minnesota was oak savanna when the first Europeans arrived in the region. We know from written accounts that the early explorers appreciated its loveliness much as people do today. Three hundred and fifty years later, less than one-tenth of one percent of the state's oak savanna remains. Dave Crawford thinks it is the scarcity of oak savanna that gives, in part, the restoration project at Wild River State Park its appeal. He says, "When you start talking about oak savanna as endangered—if we had an Endangered Habitat List, like we have an Endangered Species List—[it] would be the top item on the list, in possibly the entire world. That makes people sit back and think: 'There's something there that ought not [be lost].'"

As some recall being introduced to a person who would later become a close friend, so I remember the first time I laid eyes on preserved savanna. I instantly recognized it but simultaneously felt I had never seen anything like it before—too grassy to be a forest, too wooded to be a grassland. I realized that my childhood home of Roseville, Minnesota, had once been savanna. I had spent many days playing under the dry rustle of rusty oak leaves, in "weeds" I later learned were prairie grasses.

As a biologist, I find all natural ecosystems to be brimming with intricacy and beauty. However, only the savanna fills me with emotion that I seem unable to plumb. I return again and again to see what else the savanna has to say. I am passionate about its restoration.

I am reclining on the smooth Naugahyde-clad form of a dental chair. I have assumed the position: feet up, head back, arms resting helplessly on the leather slings. A paper bib chained around my neck, I await the ministrations of the hygienist, busy at a counter arranging the tools of her profession.

My eyes scan the featureless room, take in the row of sharp, gleaming instruments aligned on the paper napkin, scrutinize the overhead lamp with its arced and iridescent form. The walls are a bland cream color, better, I decide, than the sickly green walls of my childhood dentist, but not by much. Overhead on the ceiling, placed so I can observe it in tipped position, someone has plastered a small poster with an inspirational verse, something inane like "Sunshine Is the Song of Serenity." I don't think too hard about the words, but the image itself intrigues me. It is of a solitary bur oak silhouetted against a clear sky, field spilling off beyond the tree in all directions, the horizon unbroken where field meets sky.

It might be a savanna. It *feels* like a savanna. It is, at any rate, an oddly compelling picture, and I look and look, imagining myself in the shade of the tree, watching the wind feather the grass, staring off to the edges of the horizon.

Someone has chosen this poster for its ability to soothe, for its calming effect on people in miserable circumstances. What intrigues me is this: I doubt anyone in this office knows that environmental psychology studies show pictures of this type do exactly that—calm and soothe. Cross-cultural studies demonstrate that people respond positively to parklike environments–scenes with openness, smooth grassy vegetation, and scattered trees. People report feelings of "peacefulness" and "relaxation" after viewing them. Some studies even measure physiological characteristics like heart rate and muscle tension to show that after stress people recover more quickly when exposed to a grassy, parklike landscape.

Why this should be so, nobody knows. People embracing the idea of "biophilia"–the love of living things–claim it is because humans evolved in a savanna-like setting and our psyches are genetically imprinted to gravitate toward this type of landscape– openness, which reveals predators, and scattered trees, for shelter and protection.

This attempt to extend evolutionary theory into the realm of human psychology can only suggest a truth rather than definitively claim it. Perhaps it is all conjecture. What I do know is that the savanna marked me upon first introduction and keeps me coming back–to restore it and to be restored by it.

Yet, can we really restore anything? That is what I ask myself as I pass time in an exam room at the North Branch Clinic, awaiting the doctor. Through the high, narrow window overlooking the golf course, I study the cluster of bur oaks edging the ninth hole fairway. Can humans heal? Can we restore the inner workings of nature?

We often bring health to an ailing human body, yet any experienced physician can tick off the times he or she has prescribed treatments that have had no effect, mulled over "failure to thrive" patients who respond to nothing, scratched heads over truly sick people who have no definable symptoms. Nature presents to us an ambiguous face, full of clues we may or may not interpret rightly, if at all. It seems beyond us to probe her inner secrets. We offer medication as before a god, with a small bow: "Here–see what you will make of this."

So it seems with that larger unit of nature, an ecosystem. The land will be what it will be. A sense of this, I think, pervades the field of restoration biology, the adherents of which speak formally not of "restoring a savanna" but rather of "bringing back a particular set of influences" that were operating before massive, modern human disturbance. Some of these influences require activity on our part—frequent fires, for example, or eliminating aggressive, non-native plants. But much of it is simply letting it be—not mowing, not plowing, not logging, not paving, giving the land wide berth, freedom from our meddlesome tendencies.

Is it not unutterably human to think, in our arrogance, that we are the caregivers and Nature our submissive recipient? In actuality, the reverse is true. It is Nature, even damaged, scarred, beaten-back Nature, who restores us through offerings as subtle as a scent or a silhouette of a tree on a poster, so fully are humans and Nature meshed together. It is only our noise that deafens us to this understanding.

On an April morning, still sharp with winter's lingering trace, my daughter Christina and her third-grade classmates step into the Amador Prairie at Wild River State Park. The early settlers named this spot, but it had its oaks and one day will have them again. Before we can see savanna, we must restore prairie, and today is the day. Each child clutches an ice cream pail of prairie seeds, seeds gathered the previous fall and stored through the winter, then mixed in various amounts so that everyone carries an assortment of species. Their faces are lit with anticipation, with joy at being out of school, out in the open, in the spring. On a signal from the teachers, the children spread out into the prairie's expanse, thread their way through the straw-colored hummocks of decaying grasses, and begin to sow the seed.

The spring wind is high. It snaps at the children's jackets and tousles their hair. Christina's blond tresses loft like a halo around her face as her arm traces an arc through the air. The seeds spray outward, a half-circle of promise, before they settle onto the earth.

ACKNOWLEDGMENTS

Potato City benefited greatly from community input. The following people consented to interviews, read portions of the manuscript, and enhanced my understanding of North Branch life: the late Doris Alvin, Clayton Anderson, Tom Anderson, Roy Hammerstrom, Allan Jarchow, the late Fillmore Johnson, Thomas Johnson of Cambridge, Carl and Phyllis Lindberg, Ted Mansk, Stan and Barb Ledbetter Nelson, Gary Noren, the late Carroll Olson, Doug Swanson, Lawrence Swenson, and Tom Zeien. A special thanks to Max Malmquist, who read and commented on the entire manuscript. Whatever faults lie on these pages are mine alone.

My heartfelt thanks to past and present members of my writing group, whose insightful comments made this a better book: Andrea Bolger, Patti Isaacs, Tara McAdams, Susan Narayan, Pam Schmid, Shirley Schwarzrock, and Sharon Soderlund.

I am indebted to my teachers: Bob Esbjornson, who led me to realize I loved writing; Cheri Register, who introduced me to the craft of essay writing; and the late Paul Gruchow, who taught me to see nature in a new way.

Sherry Stirling of the Chisago County Historical Society, Marilyn McGriff of the Isanti County Historical Society, Steve Libby of 1,000 Friends of Minnesota, Dave Crawford of the Minnesota Department of Natural Resources, Rod Elmstrand of the Chisago County Extension Office, Mark D. Johnson, formerly of the Geology Department at Gustavus Adolphus College, now of the University of Gothenburg, Sweden, and Gary Meyer of the Minnesota Geological Survey all aided me with their expertise.

The sensitivity and skill of Ann Regan, managing editor, and Shannon Pennefeather, editor, at Borealis Books made this a readable book.

My parents, Paul and Dorothy Busch, opened me up to the natural world.

Lastly, Tom, Andy, Katie, John, and Christina Leaf lived some of the stories and listened to others. They made this book possible.

Potato City was designed and set in type by Will Powers at the Minnesota Historical Society Press. The type is Wessex, designed by Matthew Butterick. *Potato City* was printed by Thomson-Shore, Inc., Dexter, Michigan, on New Leaf EcoBook 100 paper, made entirely from recycled post-consumer waste paper.